BECOMING
the
Blues

BECOMING
the
Blues

A Family Memoir

DARLA BARBER, JOHN BARBER,
——— *and* ———
MAGDALENA BARBER-LECLERC

iUniverse LLC
Bloomington

BECOMING THE BLUES
A FAMILY MEMOIR

The information, ideas, and suggestions in this book are not intended as a substitute for professional medical advice. Neither the author nor the publisher shall be liable or responsible for any loss or damage allegedly arising as a consequence of your use or application of any information or suggestions in this book.

iUniverse books may be ordered through booksellers or by contacting:

iUniverse
1663 Liberty Drive
Bloomington, IN 47403
www.iuniverse.com
1-800-Authors (1-800-288-4677)

Because of the dynamic nature of the Internet, any web addresses or links contained in this book may have changed since publication and may no longer be valid. The views expressed in this work are solely those of the author and do not necessarily reflect the views of the publisher, and the publisher hereby disclaims any responsibility for them.

ISBN: 978-1-4917-0196-6 (sc)
ISBN: 978-1-4917-0198-0 (hc)
ISBN: 978-1-4917-0197-3 (e)

Library of Congress Control Number: 2013913900

Printed in the United States of America.

iUniverse rev. date: 8/29/2013

We dedicate this book to our wonderful
family and friends who love Josh so much
and who have supported us unconditionally.

CONTENTS

PREFACE

T HIS IS A BOOK ABOUT life, love, and passionate commitments. Our son/brother Josh Barber, is a treasured member of a loving and supportive family. The unique rhythms and joys of his passions and talents swept us up with his exuberance for life, and we shared both his thrills and his sorrows. In spite of eight months of repeating tailspins, this book is first and foremost a memoir of a popular musician and his family—a typical American kid succeeding through hard work and sheer talent and supported by a photogenic cast of family and friends.

In 2010, crisis after crisis accumulated to fill a dark well of despair that flooded Josh's senses and challenged his resilience and our family's strong bulwark of support. Some of his circumstances were the results of his own actions, some were made worse by trends in the culture, some were just plain chance—occasions of what we call good luck turning bad.

During that year, we discovered many things about Josh, about ourselves, about the so-called safety net of emergency and health care services, and about the culture of social media among young people. Since then, we have also given a great deal of thought to additional issues related to depression and the efficacy of counseling and pharmacological treatments. Our hope is that we can identify the gaps in services and support that might transform others' desperate feelings and help them regain their passion for life. If we can describe and understand Josh's experiences, perhaps our story can help shape improvements in services and support for others. We are just one family, but even among professionals, many agree with our assessment that the mental health care system is inadequate when it comes to treating the disorder of depression. Our perspective is focused on the experience of those who turn to this support system in abject need—when a situation is extremely dire and even the smallest of healing gestures is welcome respite from panic and imminent devastation.

Josh's encounters point to a number of significant opportunities for improvement of the essential character of mental health care services. Amidst the painful, and occasionally even harmful, treatment that he received, a number of dedicated individuals shine like beacons of hope that a better system is possible.

We doubt that Josh's story will have any impact on the swelling tide of social media, but ours is not the only story of lives ruined, in part, by the deluge of personal information available online. There are many stories about others whose lives are harmed by casual access to intimate details about other people. One by one, these cautionary tales must have an effect. In the case of our son, Facebook was a ubiquitous danger; he couldn't resist the very exposures that were guaranteed to enflame his anguish.

Our goal in writing this book is not only to tell Josh's story but to help others. We hope that reading this book will help other families realize that they are not alone. Even when you focus all your love and attention wholeheartedly on helping someone, you may have limited success. Through telling our story, we hope to inspire changes that will improve treatment for others who are struggling in similar ways. Or perhaps a spark from this book will light someone else's path to healing and recovery, or another family will find comfort and release by recognizing that many of the factors that impacted their lives were bigger than they could ever control. A crisis may seem to be about just one family, but it is also *always* about the policies, institutions, and systems of care our communities have developed over time—the ways we respond to crisis. In our case—and in many others in recent years—social media are also implicated in many potentially tragic outcomes.

All proceeds from sales of this book will be used to create a pilot program to improve transition services between hospital discharge after an inpatient psychiatric admission and the follow-up care needed for a successful re-entry to community life.

Darla Barber
John Barber
Magdalena Barber-Leclerc

ACKNOWLEDGMENTS

WRITING A BOOK IS ALWAYS a collaborative effort, and this one is more so than most. In addition to appreciating the emotional support and enhanced memory of our three-way joint authorship, we want to thank Jo Carubia for helping us through the long process of transforming our memories into this book. We also thank all of those who contributed their own anecdotes and memories to create a more complete story of these years. Rob Mushen was generous in his assistance, not just in the writing of the book but in living these experiences. Kristy Arnold, Chad Seelig, and Melissa Ceprano demonstrated their generation's loyalty and honesty as friends in their willingness to convey their thoughts and recollections. Stevie J. Smith was always there when needed and, like Josh, was always true. Professional musician Tom Ferraro composed a harmonious narrative contribution to the book, based on both musical affinities and personal wisdom. He managed to hit the high notes and the low notes.

Another set of people provided invaluable feedback on drafts of the book, helping us make it better. Without the effective comments and suggestions from these people, our story might not touch hearts in the ways we intended. Each of them read and responded from their own professional and personal skill and understanding. We appreciate these gifts of time and talent from Liz Byrne, Vincent Colapietro, Joanne Green, Susan Kennedy, Joanne Mazzotta, Kate Staley, and Evelyn Wald.

It goes without saying that we are grateful for the love and support of our families and friends over the years. Family members who are no longer alive still sustain us by the words, phrases, and gestures we remember. Even if we have not mentioned all of our siblings, cousins, nieces, and nephews by name, we recall all of the phone calls and visits, and we treasure the encouragement and love of each and every one.

The events of this book are recounted from our perspectives and to the best of our knowledge and recollection. In a few cases, names of persons have been changed when we did not have their input in describing a situation(s) involving that person. We do *not* intend to suggest blame or responsibility of any individual for the actions of others. We recognize that our knowledge of events may be partial and/or inaccurate when we were not present in person. On the larger themes of the book, we offer the viewpoint of one family and hope that it contributes for the benefit of others.

Darla Barber
John Barber
Magdalena Barber-Leclerc

"This is a book, once plain, with blank white pages. Now containing pieces, fragments, statements, times of happiness, joy, pain, sickness, rage, confusion, and every other aspect of my life. Insignificant to most, it's helped me through infinite times of turmoil. Tears have fallen on these pages."

—Joshua Adonis Barber

CHAPTER I

Island Boy

Blessings on thee, little man,
Barefoot boy, with cheek of tan!

. . .

Outward sunshine, inward joy:
Blessings on thee, barefoot boy!
John Greenleaf Whittier

I T WAS A PERFECT DAY in every way. Ten-year-old Josh Barber was not thinking about perfection, he was living it. He had two wheels under him, spinning without conscious effort down a sun-and-shade-dappled lane that seemed to whisper his name as if he owned the road, the sunshine, and all the airy tree limbs flecked with light and swaying with joy. He was full—full of time stretching out ahead of him toward a far horizon and full of the clean satisfaction of a loyal knight who has successfully battled a fiery dragon to save the kingdom. Instead of a dragon's head, however, he was carrying a huge fish.

Josh had spent the afternoon fishing, as he often did. Today he was fishing in salt water. Just yesterday, he had spent the morning at one of the small fresh-water ponds on the island. Fishing was just one degree removed from breathing and moving, and at least two degrees higher priority than eating. Sometimes it felt to him that he was a kind of water creature who lived just temporarily on land. He knew he had what others called *luck* with catching fish. In his mind, it was not luck; it was a kind of affinity. The fish seemed to want to get close to him and vice versa. If they weren't exactly jumping on shore to get to him, they did seem to choose his hook and line over any others and also over living out their lives without him.

As he pedaled with his lopsided cargo—looking and feeling quite as remarkable as a knight carrying a dragon's severed head—Josh was considering how to tell today's story. He could approach the house quietly and shush his little sister, Maggie, who was sure to shout if she saw the huge fish before noticing her brother's signal to be quiet. If he recruited Maggie to be part of a surprise presentation, he would have the double reward of another notch in her adoration plus the astonishment of his parents at the size of his catch. If he were to put his unarticulated feelings into words, Josh would admit that he didn't find Maggie at all annoying. She was the best audience a ten-year-old could want; she *always* looked up to him and not just because she was shorter. In Maggie's eyes, Josh felt like the strongest, smartest, funniest boy who ever lived. He included her in just about everything, except fishing. Maggie didn't really enjoy fishing.

Maybe Maggie just never had the chance to learn fishing the way he did as the first son and first grandson of two great fishermen, his father John and his father's father Charlie, or Poppy, as the grandchildren called him. Josh had felt central to the universe with a pole in his hand, casting and reeling in since he was about four years old. Three generations of Barber men would line up along the Yantic River and nearby ponds in Norwich, Connecticut, and with varying levels of skill, angling to catch freshwater fish, trout, catfish, and bass. Little Josh was incredibly focused on developing the skills he observed carefully in his father and grandfather. He couldn't seem to get enough of it and would ask repeatedly to go fishing, perhaps even more than appealed to the dedicated older fishermen in the family.

Island Boy

Fish Stories

When they moved to Rhode Island, Josh's passion for fishing was smoothly relocated from fresh water to the salt water bays, marshes, and open ocean within constant view of their Jamestown home. The boy was virtually defined by his fishing and the stories about his fishing that became family legends—like the one about the eight-pound bass he caught to win the Memorial Day tournament when he was just five years old.

Every year, both Darla's and John's families would gather in Maine for the Memorial Day weekend. John and his dad had been revving up Darla's family in the fishing department. The family had started a tournament a few years earlier, and by now, there was a whole ritual around the activities, including a plaque with winners'

3

names and quite a bit of competition among the men, women, and boys. There were probably three or four small groups fishing in separate boats spread out around Kezar Lake in favorite, lucky spots. John and his father had Josh in the boat with them. It was toward the end of the three-day weekend and at the most unfavorable time of day for catching fish. John felt there was nothing happening for them in the spot where they had been for the past hour. "Let's pull up and move," he said. Everything about the lake seemed asleep—the fish, the fishermen, and even the bait.

Josh and his Poppy were fishing with rubber worm lures, and John, idly contemplating what strategy to try next, decided to relieve himself in the lake. Not two minutes later, Josh was jerked forward as his pole bent over from a vigorous pull on the line. This was no little tug or nibble; this was a huge fish hooked securely at the opposite end of the pole from a five-year-old! "Dad! Poppy! I got one!"

There was a good bit of shouting and rocking of the boat as the two men resisted the impulse to grab the pole from the little boy, all the while keeping their strong hands on both him and the pole. They coached Josh and kept a close watch to be sure he wasn't pulled out of the boat in the struggle. He was tough. After what seemed to be forever, he reeled in an eight-pound bass from the lake that had given up, at most, four pounds to every other tournament winner. John's brothers-in-law claimed that he "chummed in" the big fish with his bio-waste, and that got the biggest laugh of the day.

Mostly, everyone was in complete awe at the unheard-of feat achieved by a boy who hadn't even started school yet. There was a big buzz of comments:

"You've got to keep it! What a trophy!"

"Yeah, don't release that one. It's a keeper!"

John's seemed to be the only voice counseling the opposite. "No, we should let him go."

Despite his certainty of the right course of action, he wanted his son to make the decision, so he attached a chain to the fish and anchored it to the dock so that it could swim in the water while they debated.

Over the next hour, adults were distracted by cooking chores and embellishing the story over a few beers, while Josh stayed a while to watch his fish, and then went off to play with his cousins. Sometime later, John went out to check on the fish. He pulled on the chain and up came only half a fish! The turtles had enjoyed a free meal! John made sure that the remaining front half of the fish was cleaned and mounted in a very dramatic posture, coming straight out of the mounting board with mouth wide open as if still jumping for the rubber worm. It hung in Josh's room for his entire childhood and adolescence.

Prize winning 8 pound bass at age 5

Josh loved to recall the moment when he felt that big fish tug on his line! It made him feel like some kind of superhero, the ordinary kid that everyone was watching to see him transform into a bolt of lightning, stop a speeding train, or land a humongous fish. Every new fish brought it back, and he aimed higher and higher to get the same reaction from his parents. Now, riding home with yet another big fish, he pondered how to make the most of today's fine catch.

If he didn't see Maggie as he approached the house, he might just sneak up on his mom and surprise her. Darla was always a good mark for some prank because she loved him so, so much. He could tell that his mother loved Maggie in a way that made her want to keep the little girl right by her side. She loved Josh differently; she encouraged him to be brave in the world and have adventures, but she was also alert to any danger that might come his way, like a mother bear watching over her cubs as they roam the woods. Josh knew that his mother was ferocious and would kill to protect him.

One morning, when Josh was about six years old and still small enough to live within his mother's protective custody, he set off Darla's "Mama Bear" alarm. The little boy had awakened in the quiet moment between John leaving for work and Darla rising to start her day with the children. A compelling mental image of some spectacular catch was pulling at him, and he wrote his mother a note, "GON FISIN," before leaving the house to pursue his goal. When Darla found the note in Josh's large, tilted letters, she ran outside to look for him. His fishing pole and sneakers were gone from beside the front door.

After calling the neighbors and shouting for Josh up and down the road and along the beach just in front of the house, Darla phoned John at work and contacted the local police. A single-minded, fishing-obsessed, six-year-old boy was at large somewhere on the island or deep in the waters surrounding it.

As a few neighbors arrived and spread out to search the area, Darla was nearly hysterical with anxiety. She knew her son's spirit. He would follow a fish as far as he could and sometimes a little farther. He didn't hesitate one instant to think about danger, but danger was all his mother could see. In her mind, every minute meant another jagged rock or surging wave endangering her son. In less than an hour, Josh was discovered ambling over beach rocks and driftwood, pushing north, single-mindedly in search of the very best spot to angle for treasure.

Being "lost" made little impression on Josh. He was quite confident that he knew where he was at all times, and after a million hugs from his mother and the short fuss over his being "missing," he was just as determined to continue fishing at every possible opportunity. On foot, on his bike, with friends, with Dad or alone, fishing was number one with Josh. At this age, he could spend entire days, accompanied by Darla and little Maggie, at Heads Beach, just down the road from the house, hauling all sorts of things out of the ocean. Fish and quahogs were guaranteed, but there would be occasional blue crabs and lobsters, too. If he got tired of the ocean (almost never) or just wanted a change of scenery, Josh would fish one of the freshwater ponds on the island for the huge largemouth bass that must have been lurking there for decades.

Pedaling home with his perfect specimen, Josh cycled through these and other fishing "legends" that he loved to hear repeated. He never intended to make a legend—they just seemed to happen. What felt ordinary to him, he realized, might have seemed brighter or bigger or louder to others. Josh saw that there were big fish, but he also saw big dragons in the world and when he did, he stood his ground and kept reeling. He sometimes even picked up the sword sticking out of a nearby stone. Maggie, Darla, and John were always there as first and best audience or, when needed, as first responders for any dragons he couldn't handle alone. On this particular day, Darla saw him coming from a distance and before he could surprise her, she grabbed a camera to capture the boy balanced between the past and the future in one perfect moment.

CHAPTER II

Intensity in a Small Package

his voice is green like growing (is miraculous like
tomorrow) . . . since he's young with mysteries . . .

e.e.cummings

I N LATE 1979, JOHN AND Darla Barber made lists of boys and girls names for the baby they were expecting in March of the following year. John suggested the name "Waylon." Darla wrote it on the list to humor him, but she was far from crazy about it. Waylon Jennings was a country singer, and John had never been a country music fan. How did he come up with that name?

Joshua Adonis Barber was born on March 21, 1980. He was a full-term baby but very tiny—just five pounds, six ounces. Darla had been a model of expectant motherhood; she restricted her caffeine consumption and didn't smoke or drink alcohol during the pregnancy. It was a normal pregnancy until the very last weeks. Her doctor noticed that her ankles were swelling, so he instructed her to stay in bed and cut back on salt in her diet. She followed his orders precisely.

Within a couple of days, things had gotten worse, and a very worried John brought Darla to the hospital with an unbearable headache. One of the doctors from the obstetrics and gynecology practice entered her room to examine her. After stuttering for a moment with a look of dismay on his face, he blurted out, "You know what I'm going to do for you? I'm going to give you a couple of Tylenol!"

Not for a minute did they believe that he had even a clue of what to do as he bounced back and forth like a shy schoolboy. Darla's head was throbbing.

As if Darla were in a coma or completely unaware of her actions, a nurse would come in to take vital signs, and she would sigh, roll her eyes, and shake her head as she recorded Darla's blood pressure. But Darla *was* aware of what was going on minute by minute. She was aware of blood being drawn for multiple blood tests, and she heard the diagnosis of preeclampsia. She heard them say that her organs were shutting down and that her sister Candace, who had come from New Hampshire for the birth, should get to the hospital immediately if she wanted to see Darla. Through all of this, Darla focused on the tiny heart beating beneath her own. She was silently encouraging her child, "Stay with us! We're going to be OK! We'll get through this together!"

When Dr. Watson arrived, things started to turn around. He made sure that Darla drank several small cups of tomato juice laced with salt; he ordered an ultrasound to check on the baby's size and position; and he announced the intent of inducing labor early the next morning. Dr. Watson had a calming effect, and Darla and John felt reassured that everything was appropriately under control.

That evening, the third doctor in the practice entered Darla's room to give the young couple the results of the ultrasound and the plan for the next day. Among many other details of his report, he said the ultrasound showed *intrauterine growth retardation*. When John asked the doctor what that meant, he replied, "Well, I can't promise you that your baby won't come out looking like this," and he gestured with his arms and body twisted and contorted.

Throughout the entire conversation, this physician was juggling balls at the foot of Darla's bed. They were completely horrified by his comments and gestures! Even in the very best of circumstances, having their first child is a stressful event for a young couple. This family was going through an extreme situation under the care of two out of three doctors who either didn't understand the condition or, who, perhaps despite some outstanding technical prowess, had no ability to communicate in an emotionally supportive manner. John called the family to let them know what the doctor had stated. Needless to say, it was a sleepless night for many in the Barber extended family, with abundant tears shed. *Intrauterine growth retardation*, as they all found out much later, simply means that the baby is small.

The delivery the next morning, to everyone's relief, was uncomplicated. Indeed, Josh was small, but he was healthy and perfectly formed. John and Darla put their fears behind them and concentrated on getting acquainted with their son.

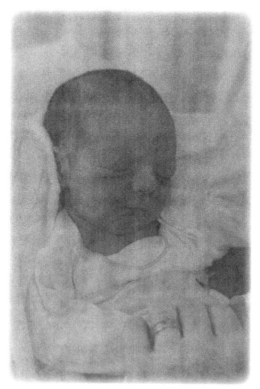

Joshua Adonis Barber

Welcome to the Family

The Barbers were living in Norwich, Connecticut, at the time of Josh's birth. John was working toward being an American success story from the time of his first position in the maintenance department at the Navy's "First and Finest Submarine Base" in New London. When this young man said, "Yes, I can," it was a guarantee that the job would get done properly and in good time. He took every opportunity to get further training to better himself, and soon he was building torpedoes. He was precise and thoughtful, paid attention to the details, and could deliver a report in crisp, clear language. It wasn't long before he was inspecting torpedo maintenance facilities, and eventually he was asked to join the team that travels around the world re-certifying facilities in other countries. In 1980, John was at the very beginning of this trajectory. He was twenty-six years old, and Darla was twenty-five.

Darla was inspired, even in her youth, to give her heart and her hands to care for others. She was a home health aide when she worked outside the home in the years before their children went to school, and after the children were grown, she continued her own education to become a registered nurse. She was thrilled to become a mother and enjoyed every day at home with Josh and then three years later, with Maggie and Josh.

Josh was a happy baby. He often sported an amazingly broad grin, from ear to ear, just like his Grampy Snow, Darla's dad. He was a charismatic baby. John's mother, Josh's Yia Yia—Greek, for grandmother—would often say, "He sends me!" It was love at first sight between Josh and his Yia Yia, and there was a very special connection between John's father, Poppy, and Josh as well.

In hindsight, this little baby boy was also very intense. In the photo albums from these years, there are many snapshots of baby Josh with a furrowed brow. He didn't look angry but as though he was really concentrating, trying to figure things out, perhaps more than the camera could capture. He was a charismatic and intense baby who would grow up to be a charismatic and intense man.

A grandchild often brings married couples closer to their own parents. In the Barber family, this became true in a very tangible way. Darla and John bought from his parents the house in Norwich where John grew up. John's parents, Charlie and Stasia—or Poppy and Yia Yia—bought the house next door, connected through the backyards. Only a field and a stone wall divided the two properties, and soon there was a gap in the stone wall wide enough for a little boy to walk through. Poppy and Yia Yia kept chickens, and there were always fresh eggs for breakfast.

As soon as he could walk and talk, Josh and Yia Yia would get on the phone first thing in the morning. Sometimes she would say, "Come on up for a dippin' egg!" or Josh would say, "I'm coming up for a dippin' egg." He would march up through the field, his mother watching from one house and his grandmother receiving him at the other. She made him a fresh, over-easy egg for dipping his toast into the bright, creamy yolk. Josh and Yia Yia kept this ritual almost every day, weather permitting. They were extremely close.

It was the same with John's dad. Poppy taught Josh to fish, and they would go fishing together from the time he was a little boy. If Josh wasn't over at Poppy's and Yia Yia's, they were at his house or in his yard. They were always together.

Little Josh and his mother were also very close. Stasia would say to Darla, "He's so attached to you! He's attached at the hip."

Darla knew they were close; they were together all the time. When Josh went to nursery school at around three years old, he resisted the separation from his mother. Josh and his cousin Anastasia were the same age, and they started at Park Nursery School at the same time. As Anastasia was set down from her mother's arms, she would scurry along, happy to play with the toys and other children. Josh seemed terrified. Almost every day that Darla dropped him off, he would cling to her and cry. She would go home with an upset stomach. Typically, the teacher would call Darla not more than half an hour later, saying, "He's just fine; he's calmed down and is playing happily now." Still, to his mother, he seemed a little more anxious than other kids.

Josh was just about to have his third birthday when his little sister Magdalena was born on March 7, 1983. Right from the start, he was tuned in to the little bundle of pink and white. He would run to Darla or John when Maggie cried, saying "Baby's crynin! Baby's crynin!" Big brother already had a compassionate heart and wanted to bring comfort to the little one in distress. There is a recording of three-year old Josh calling the radio station to announce, "I have a new baby sista!" When they asked the baby's name, he proudly stated, "My baby sista, Maggie!"

In 1985, John was offered a position at the Naval Undersea Warfare Center (NUWC) in Newport, Rhode Island. This was a good opportunity for him to advance his career, and the Barbers decided as a family that he would accept the offer and they would move to Rhode Island.

The municipality of Newport, with a population of 24,672 at the 2010 census, is located on Aquidneck Island. Best known in this century as a summer vacation destination with music festivals, beaches, museums, restaurants, gifts shops, and much more, it has been notable since its founding in 1639 as a site of religious freedom, as a major shipping commerce center, as a focal point of summer society for the wealthy, and as "The Sailing Capital of the World." Newport is also the home of a major United States Navy base (Naval Station Newport), including the Naval War College, the Naval Justice School, various training facilities, and the Naval Undersea Warfare Center. In 2009, when the NUWC celebrated 140 years of continuous operation, a press release summarized the history of the facility: "The Newport Torpedo Station was founded on Goat Island in the Newport, RI., harbor in July 1869 and retained its original name until 1951. For the next 15 years, it was the Underwater Ordinance Station, and then the Underwater Weapons Research and Engineering Station until 1970. That year, the Underwater Sound

Lab from New London, Conn., was combined with the Newport facility to form the Naval Underwater Systems Center or NUSC. In 1992, the command was reorganized as the Naval Undersea Warfare Center, Division Newport."

A New Home

John and Darla wanted to settle in a family-friendly community, and they considered several locations within an easy commute of Newport. Once they had explored Jamestown, however, it was no contest. The community is leisurely spread out over Conanicut Island, nine miles long and just one mile across at its widest point. With a top elevation of 135 feet, the island is connected to the mainland—North Kingstown to the west and Newport to the east—by two graceful spans and is still mostly wooded, with a number of working farms and a picturesque village center on the water where sunrise is gently lifted by sailboat masts and fairy-lighted bridge towers. An historic windmill (1787) anchors the place in time, and a mostly year-round population of about 6,000 residents supports a few trendy cafés and restaurants, a well-stocked hardware store, elementary and junior high schools, and a modern library. You can walk to the water and spectacular views from anyplace on the island.

The young family spent many hours driving the narrow roads up, down, and across the island, looking for potential homes for sale or rent in their price range. One afternoon as they checked out Seaside Drive, they noticed a brand new, solar-efficient, salt-box home directly on Narragansett Bay. There was a "For Rent" sign on the lawn. Darla remembers that moment clearly, "We knew we couldn't possibly afford this beautiful home, but we couldn't help thinking, 'Wouldn't it be great if we could live HERE!'" John decided that, even though it was a long shot, it was certainly worth their time to inquire about renting this house. At the very least, they would be able to tour the inside of the house and savor their dream of one day having a home like this for themselves. The rent, they learned, was $1,200 a month, at least double what they could afford!

The Hobbs family was at home when John and Darla came to see the house, and Darla's heart went out to their young daughter with special needs. She sat on the floor to connect at eye level with the child and immediately engaged her in play. The girl responded to Darla's warmth, and there was a quiet pause as the other adults watched. At the end of the visit, Mr. Hobbs said that they would be happy if the Barbers decided to live in their home for $650 per month—a small miracle inspired by a big heart.

The Barber family moved on the auspicious date of John's birthday, March 3, 1985. They had left a lovely setting among family in Norwich, and they were feeling extremely fortunate with the new horizons opening ahead of them.

Josh was turning five and Maggie was two. They were learning to roller skate outside on the smooth, wide boards of the wrap-around deck, surrounded by water and sky. John was totally engaged in establishing himself at the new job. Darla was mission control for all their lives, and, in addition, she was the point person on a search for their *own* house. She made the calls, followed up on the leads, and went out to see a few possibilities. Everything that they liked was very expensive and beyond their means. The search was expanded to include finding a building lot. They could build their own home for about the same price or even less than the homes they were seeing, and then they would have exactly what they wanted. While John was at work, Darla would drive around looking for a piece of land that might have potential and writing letters to the owners. After many months of searching, she discovered a beautiful corner building lot almost in their back yard, just one street up the hill away from the water. It would be perfect!

Darla went to the town clerk's office and found out who owned the property. When she and John contacted the owners, they learned that this couple was building their own dream home in Martha's Vineyard. Someone had given them the property in Jamestown as a wedding gift. One of them wanted to sell it, and the other didn't. The Barbers assumed that it was not going to work out, and they returned to their search. About two months later, Darla got a phone call that the owners had decided to sell them the property.

The Barber family bought the land and cleared it themselves. They inquired about the designer of another Jamestown house that they loved, and then they created the plans for their home with that architect's help. The framing was hired out and went quickly, and then John did all the plumbing and electrical work and almost everything else himself.

Childhood Escapades

Meanwhile, Josh was starting kindergarten at the Lawn Avenue School in Jamestown. For most children, starting school is a big step, not only up into that big school bus but out into a bigger world with unfamiliar faces, unknown places, new routines, and lots and lots of rowdy kids. Josh was a fairly typical kid for his age; some days he went eagerly to school, and some days he just didn't want to go at all. He would be completely ready to go, with his backpack on, waiting outside with one of his parents, but when the bus came, he would say, "I don't want to go to school!"

"You have to go to school," would be the calm response, and they would go back and forth like this a few times before he reluctantly got on the bus.

One day, Josh was particularly determined not to go to school. He was outside waiting for the bus as usual, but just when the bus stopped, he bolted around to the back of the house. Darla quickly followed him but not quickly enough. By the time she came around the corner, he had climbed up into an empty rabbit cage and swung the door shut. The wire mesh cage was quite small and built up on sturdy poles about three feet off the ground so the dogs couldn't get to it. She laughed and laughed at the site of her little kindergartener

16

hunched like a bunny inside the cage up off the ground against the blue background of the sky and Narragansett Bay! Even in that moment, she knew this would become a favorite family story to tell over and over.

The story of little Josh in the rabbit cage was very funny, but it was also the beginning of a realization that he was starting to have a little of what his pediatrician called *school anxiety*. John and Darla thought that perhaps he was having trouble with the bigger kids on the bus. Josh was quite small, even compared with other kindergarten kids. As his resistance to getting on the bus continued, the parents spoke to several teachers. There definitely were some seventh and eighth graders who occasionally tormented smaller kids, but apparently they weren't bothering Josh specifically. The overall roughhousing on the bus might have made him nervous, and sometimes he was better able to cope with it, sometimes not. When he was going through a bad spell, his doctor would say again, "Oh, he just has school anxiety."

John and Darla tried to deal with it on a day-to-day basis simply as a stage of development that Josh would outgrow. The combined factors of being smaller than other kids his age, along with anxiety and aversion to school busses, would return from time to time as a puzzle that would finally be solved a few years later.

Meanwhile, Josh was an active, happy, and successful kid both in and out of school. Like Tom Sawyer and Huck Finn on the Mississippi, the Boxcar Children, and Eloise at the Plaza, Josh Barber's childhood was a classic American tale. All of the elements add up to a perfect "chapter book" for new readers: a picturesque and unspoiled setting typical of northeast coastal America; a childhood of fantasy play, scrapes and stitches with the little sister in pigtails; and lots of dramatic challenges and conflicts with both environmental and human protagonists!

Josh was barely in school and Maggie little more than a sturdy toddler when the Barbers cleared the property and hired out the foundation work on their new home. The kids played in the mountains of dirt while their parents inspected concrete and envisioned the

17

bulk of the house and the sweep of the landscaping. Josh stamped and packed dirt into rough steps so he and Maggie and their buddy Kristy Arnold could climb to the top of the loose piles and gain a little better perspective on the scene. Instead of being blocked by even small bushes and looking up to just about everything, they could be pirates looking outward to spot whales, sharks, and enemies at sea. Or they could look down and see the patterns of their parents and the workers doing what grown-ups do all day long. The final advantage of climbing to the top of a dirt mountain is the tremendous rush of catapulting down, heedless of grimy stained clothes and filthy rings around their necks, ankles, wrists, and eventually, the bathtub.

Dirt mountains were just one small, temporary attraction of the neighborhood. A huge rock on the nearby beach was the focus of infinite imaginative play. Kristy joined the siblings for a game that went on for several seasons. She described their roles:

> Josh pretended to be the dad, me the mom, and Maggie the baby. The whale rock was our home, but it was also a giant whale that we had to feed mashed up periwinkles lest the shark would attack the whale, putting our family in danger. Josh, the dad, would need to hunt and gather the periwinkles, and we crushed them inside the whale's mouth before the shark came in with the tide! I put the baby (Maggie) to bed on the baby whale (a smaller rock next to the whale rock) . . . The excitement grew as the tide came in with the dangerous shark.

The three friends were inseparable in summer; long days of playing in the dirt, climbing on the rocks, or swinging on a rope would often end with dinner at one another's homes. One day, according to Kristy, who was the older child, the two girls "had a brilliant idea to pee in a bucket in Mr. Egan's shed." Afterwards, Josh told them that he had witnessed the deed and that he was going to tell their parents. The two little girls were speechless at the thought of their parents finding out what they had done! The years since have cast these actions in a different light, and smiles, rather than shock, come to their faces at the memories.

Sometimes, even such innocent play morphed into danger, and Josh had the bloody shirt to prove it. One afternoon, he and his friends Rippie and Stanley were playing in the nearby woods, building things as active nine and ten-year olds will do. Stanley picked up a large, sharp piece of slate and heaved it through the air. He wasn't aiming at anyone; he just threw it randomly. The projectile hit Josh in the temple, right next to his eye, and severed some arteries. Josh put his hand up to the site of the sudden pain. When the hand came away covered with blood, his immediate reaction was to run after the kid who had thrown the rock. The two boys raced one after the other up the street. They reached Rippie's house first, where his mom Michelle, a good friend of Darla's and John's, screamed at the sight of Josh in a white tee-shirt covered in blood from the pulsing arteries. She quickly took charge of the situation and got the boys in the car.

John and Darla were sitting quietly at home when Michelle pulled into their driveway furiously honking the horn. Darla looked out the window and could see the white towel that Michelle was holding up against Josh's head. A decision was made to take Josh to the doctor's office in Jamestown, rather than to drive much farther to reach the nearest hospital emergency room. Darla called ahead, and they transferred Josh to their own car.

Both parents controlled their frantic impulses, getting Josh into the car while keeping pressure on the gash with the clean cloth. John drove, and Darla sat in the back with Josh. Doctor Hurley went right to work when they arrived. He gave Josh a shot of Novocain into the wound, then he clamped, cauterized, and stitched both of the arteries, and finally, he finished closing the long, deep cut.

Josh was brave through all the repairs—no tears. His main concerns were saving the shirt and keeping the rock. He thought it was pretty cool that he had a souvenir bloodstained tee-shirt. The big, heavy piece of shale had a place of honor on the deck of the Barber home for many years. It evolved from an accidental weapon into a family conversation piece. Josh was a seasoned warrior, and these were his badges of honor.

Stanley's mom Julie escorted him over to the Barber house the next day and supervised his apology. Josh shrugged it off. "It was an accident!" he said, and the incident never interfered with the friendship between the two boys.

In many ways, Josh could be said to have had a charmed life during much of his childhood and youth. His parents were firm with him, but it was clear that they cherished his exuberant spirit. Darla may have frowned and sighed, and John may have shouted or gestured with alarm during each of his many adventures, but these were short periods of parental gravity followed by their usual encouragement and solidarity. Josh was the focus of a great deal of love and support. If little Maggie wasn't part of the adventure herself, she looked up to her brother as someone she would follow no matter what the danger!

Robert Frost begins a famous poem, "Some say the world will end in fire; some say in ice." Coincidentally, young Josh Barber might have agreed. A camp on Kezar Lake in Lovell, Maine, owned by Darla's sister and her husband, was the site of at least two episodes of Josh's education with fire and ice. Kezar Lake, reportedly described in both *National Geographic* and the *New York Times* as one of the most beautiful lakes in the world, is surrounded by woods. When he wasn't fishing on the lake, Josh would often be exploring in the woods, trying out the limits of nature in a variety of ways. It might be climbing trees or trying to fashion a trap for any small animal or bird, or it might be trying to start a fire by focusing the sun's rays through a piece of glass.

One afternoon, the adults were talking and laughing inside the "camp" when Josh burst in and shouted, "Fire!" He made no excuses or apologies; he was frightened beyond fibbing at what he had done. The adults followed him out into the woods where no vehicle could have gone. They were horrified to see flames among the brush and small trees in a circle perhaps ten feet across. With blankets, shovels, and buckets of water scooped from the lake, they managed to beat back the disaster and put out the fire. If Josh had hesitated or tried to avoid the situation entirely by running to hide instead of to get help, Kezar Lake would have been circled by a ring of charred wood instead of emerald green.

Josh's encounter with ice on Kezar Lake was chilling in a quite different way. The scene was just like a Currier and Ives print of winter in New England. The lake was entirely frozen over and solid enough for small vehicles and fishing parties and even for small campfires built right on the ice. Each group cut holes through the ice to let down their baited lines and pull up the perch, bass, and whatever else took the bait. John, his father, and Josh's uncle Steven led a family group across the lake on skimobiles to set up their fishing site on the ice. Darla and Maggie stayed back at the cabin on this particularly cold day. Josh was about eight, old enough to drive the skimobile short distances at slow speeds, so long as his father kept an eye on him. If there was one thing that might distract Josh from fishing, it was driving the skimobile.

The group had set their tip-ups, devices used to hold the fishing reel and launch a spring-loaded flag when a fish bites. Everyone was close to shore, cooking hot dogs and watching for one of the flags to go up in the distance. When a couple of flags went up, all but Josh jumped on skimobiles to check on them. He was too interested in his hot dog.

John kept looking back at Josh approximately 200 yards away. He could see that Josh had had enough of the food and was running out to join in the excitement with the others. John remembers watching Josh on the run, heading straight toward him and then the unforgettable image of his body dropping out of sight, through the ice.

John alerted everyone, and all ran to where he disappeared. Uncle Steven, who was positioned near a skimobile, used the machine to get to Josh first.

A father's worst fear in this situation would be that his boy would slip down and slide sideways under the ice. If he simply falls and rises in a straight line, he will surface at the same hole. If not, he could very quickly be lost under the thick ice in any direction. Josh was clinging to the side of the hole when Steven reached down and snatched him from the hole. Everyone dashed to their skimobiles to rush him back to camp.

Darla heard the revved-up sound of the engines, not the usual leisurely drone at the end of a good fishing day, but a higher pitched and much louder roar. John carried an icy, shivering, soaked Josh into the house, and they quickly stripped him down and warmed him. By the time everyone settled in front of the fire after dinner, they were laughing about the incident, but no one could quite set aside the thought of how close they had been to a devastating outcome.

The stories they told around the fire that night centered on Josh and his intense passion for fishing. Falling through the ice would become just one brief tale in his long love affair with any experience involving fishing.

Fishing was a participation sport for men and boys in the Barber family. Darla and Maggie were more often in the role of observers or photographers. As Josh got a little older, he and John often went out in a fifteen-foot aluminum boat that they kept on a trailer, ready for action at a moment's notice. It was not unusual in the early morning or late afternoon for one of them to notice bluefish jumping in the bay. From the vantage point of their deck, they could see schools of these large fish churning the otherwise calm water in a vigorous feeding frenzy. They would double-check the phenomenon through the telescope and then run to hook the boat trailer to the truck, drive down the street about a hundred yards to launch the boat, and be fishing within minutes. "We would speed out and then be floating in the middle of an acre of hundreds of fish leaping out of the water, striking at anything we threw out there. We used plugs and caught them one after another; it didn't take long to fill the bottom of the boat. They are ferocious fighters, so it was a real rush for me and Josh."

John's description of the scene is confirmed by a photo that Darla took of the two of them standing in the boat with fish all around their ankles. On some occasions, other Jamestown residents would be waiting when they returned to the island. Father and son would hand the heavy harvest, one by one, to their neighbors, before heading home with four or five fish for their own freezer. They shared the work of flushing out the motor and then cleaning and cutting up the fish. From the time he could handle a knife safely, Josh had stepped up to the plate on the messy chore of cleaning fish. He had a young biologist's curiosity about interior anatomy and for his first few years of fishing, he would slice open the stomach of his catch to see what they had recently eaten. Fishing may be considered a leisure activity, but in many ways, it is as complete an education in the natural world as any college course. In addition, along with his initiation into the tools and skills of a fisherman, John and his father coached Josh in the personal traits of endurance, patience, initiative, sharp observation, and stamina. From the time he was a small-for-his-age five-year-old, Josh was fully engaged in demanding physical challenges on an almost daily basis. He was quite an independent child in many ways, and he grew to become a strong and somewhat daring youth.

The trust between father and son was a central factor in the development of the boy's confidence. Another fishing tale shows the depth of this trust. There was a period in his early teens when Josh and John went fishing nearly every night. Often they would take the boat to fish for striped bass in the waters off Beavertail State Park at the south end of the island. The minimum legal length to keep striped bass is twenty-eight inches. Each angler is allowed to keep only two of these fish, still a pretty impressive haul.

One night, they had caught their limit and were just turning the boat toward home when the fog set in. This particular night, they were in a fifteen-foot aluminum boat with no navigational equipment except for a small compass. It was getting late, and soon the fog was compounded by darkness. They didn't even have a light on the boat to warn others of their proximity. John kept the motor on the slowest speed, kept the boat headed north, and kept his mounting concerns to himself. Josh was sitting toward the midsection of the boat, eyes forward, musing on the eerie beauty of the foggy night. He was not frightened in the least as his father navigated in the pitch dark fog. Without seeing a single landmark, they traveled silently and slowly north for well over an hour with the guidance of the little compass. All of a sudden, over their heads, the lights from the Jamestown Bridge burned through the fog. They were dead center of the channel under the huge structure. "Son of a gun! We hit it perfectly!" John was well aware of all the potential hazards they had avoided by a narrow margin. But Josh had never questioned for a split-second his father's ability to pilot them safely home. Arriving at the familiar neighborhood landmark was just another "Yeah. So?" moment for him, nothing out of the ordinary—just Dad doing what Dad always did, keeping him safe from harm.

CHAPTER III

Hot on Ice

A good hockey player plays where the puck is.
A great hockey player plays where the puck is going to be.
Wayne Gretzky

IN THE SAGA OF BARBER family members and friends, Josh is a perpetually passionate person. He was born with an intense expression on his face, and scarcely a person failed to mention it when describing him throughout his life. Long-time family friend and Josh's mentor, Rob Mushen, said, "The one thing I discovered about Josh right away was his passion for things—hockey was a passion, art was a passion, music became a passion—even his hairstyles were passionate! But the thing he was most passionate about was people, and that passion transcended and superimposed itself on all the others. Even as a child, he could be profound, and I always found him irresistible in that way."

If Josh's passions were unfolded in a long, wide ribbon, fishing would be among the earliest of them. Compassion for others would be a solid line all along the entire length. Ice hockey would overlap fishing for a few years and would extend for a long period as one of the most significant commitments of his life.

Josh played soccer along with all the other kids in Jamestown, but when they moved on to other sports like baseball, he wasn't interested.

He had identified a hero and wanted to pursue the quintessential New England sport of ice hockey.

Josh's older cousin Shannon, whom he adored, was the captain of the women's hockey team at Boston College. Craig Janney, a Boston College star who was playing for the Boston Bruins (1987-1992), was her idol, and that was good enough for Josh. He jumped on the bandwagon, and soon the TV in the Barber household was tuned into Boston Bruins games with Josh within striking distance of the screen, absorbing every move of Craig Janney's winning style. He pestered his father to take him to games and hang around afterwards to meet Janney and get his autograph. He adopted his cousin's idol "hook, line, and sinker" and soon became determined to play the game himself.

Jamestown didn't have a hockey program, so the Barbers registered Josh in CLCF, Cranston League for Cranston's Future, a strong league that trained countless young players for fifty-five years until its dissolution in May, 2011. The coach at the entry level, where the main goal is skill building, was an ex-Boston Bruin named Bill Bennett. His family was quite famous locally for producing three Bruins.

John recalls the sight of his son on the ice that very first day. "We showed up from Jamestown and didn't know anybody. Most of the other kids knew each other. Josh was wearing these old, beat-up, limp leather skates with double runners. He was dressed in jeans and a football helmet. I looked out on the ice, and all these rich kids were out there wearing hundreds of dollars of hockey equipment. Josh skated onto the ice and just played his heart out. That first day he was falling all over the place!" John observed his son's courage and then walked up to the coach and said, "He really wants to play."

At the second practice, Bill Bennett skated over to John, and said, "This kid has so much passion for the sport, so much heart. You've got to get him some good skates. The rest of it can come later," he said. "But you've got to give him some real skates."

At the time, John wasn't earning a generous salary. He had two young children and was still laboring on the lower rungs of the career ladder. Making the time to drive up to Cranston every day was already a sacrifice for the whole family. Still, they found a way to get Josh a good pair of skates, and it wasn't long before Bill Bennett really took a liking to him.

"Look at all these kids," Bennett would say to John. "They're skating around, throwing the puck at each other, and whacking around with their sticks. Josh is out there, completely focused on learning the skills of the game. He is always challenging himself, and I see him getting better day by day."

By the beginning of his second year, he was as good as the rest of them. Bennett would sometimes start him at center, Craig Janney's position. Josh patterned his style of hockey after Janney, often going after the assist to help someone else score the goal. His name began to appear in news briefs on the results of CLCF "Squirt" (ages 9 and 10) competitions. "Despite an opening goal scored by Josh Barber with an assist from Doug Greaves, the North Stars were able to break through CLCF's defensive strategy . . . Ben Jague, Josh Barber and Albert Huang led the assault on the Providence Capitals."

Josh was small and thin for his age when he started playing hockey. He appeared much bigger in uniform, and his parents wondered how he carried all that extra weight. He would get knocked around during every game, but nothing stopped him, and soon he learned to throw some good hits himself. In every way, this small-framed youngster seemed healthy, and though adults noticed his frequent sprints for the bathroom, it was thought that he was simply responding to the excitement coming his way on game days (and sometimes on school days, too). When a school counselor suggested a complete physical to rule out any underlying medical conditions, they discovered that Josh had serious lactose intolerance. Of course, he had been drinking his milk three times a day just like every other kid in America. For this kid, however, it meant frequent upset stomach and GI disturbances. At the awards ceremony after his first season, in addition to other commendations, Josh was given a good-natured award for knowing the location of every bathroom in Rhode Island! He was always on the lookout because he often had an urgent need. On a lactose-free diet, Josh began putting on weight and feeling much better on the school bus and while traveling to his hockey games. His additional size continued to fuel his success in hockey. His passing game grew stronger, and his overall style became more aggressive.

Josh's passion for hockey was contagious. He and his friend Ben Butterfield started playing street hockey in Jamestown on the afternoons when Josh wasn't at practice, and soon Ben joined CLCF, too. John or Darla, or both of them plus Maggie, would drive Ben and Josh to practice at least forty minutes away in Cranston, and sometimes even further for games when he moved up from playing club hockey within the league to the travel team playing as far away as New York or Martha's Vineyard. They would sit and watch the practice or game and then drive the athletes home. Ben was a couple of years older than Josh and had introduced him to the band called *Bush*. On the way to a game, John would play their hit song "Machinehead" full blast while the boys shouted along to the lyrics in the back seat. John described this experience from a parent's point of view as "two kids all outfitted in their hockey equipment rocking to the music!"

The Barbers became a hockey family. Darla and John were overjoyed to see Josh thriving on the ice, and little Maggie was a consistently good sport about having her life revolve around hockey. Josh's obvious talent and mania for the game carried the whole family into the hockey world, and they loved it. One year, when Maggie was old enough to be a Mini Mite, she donned the gear and gave it a try, but playing the game wasn't the thrill for her that it was for Josh. She was wobbly and adorable, with her long blond hair showing below the helmet, but she decided that playing in the stands with the other hockey siblings was a lot more entertaining! She never felt that she was missing out on anything in a tight-knit family devoted in these years to her brother's talents. "I remember spending a lot of time as a child in hockey rinks. I never minded being dragged around to all different ice rinks. It was fun to watch Josh play; it was fun to be with the other families. It was like a little community."

Off the Ice

Josh was a regular popular kid in Jamestown. At all the right times, he did all the typical things: selling lemonade, riding bikes, having sleepovers and pillow fights, playing Marco Polo in summer, and going sledding in winter. Maggie remembers her brother as "goofy and funny" in his young teen years. In addition, she says, "Josh was a big Jim Carrey fan. He loved Jim Carrey's crazy sense of humor. I remember watching *Ace Ventura* (1994) over and over with him. A couple of years later, Jim Carrey came to Jamestown to film part of *Me, Myself and Irene*. Josh and I played hooky from school and went downtown to watch them film. He came around and signed autographs, and we have pictures from that day of Josh and Jim Carrey together."

Josh was a decent student in elementary and middle school, with no spectacular report card grades in either direction. Writing and the arts were clearly his stronger subjects, and math was most definitely not. He hated math. He hated the grueling homework sessions with his father. They sat together at the dining room table, but only one of them was focused on the numbers. "You are getting these grades working at only 50% of your ability! Just think what you can do if you give it 100% effort!"

John Barber was an equal opportunity parent when it came to effort at school. Maggie, coming home with A's on her report card, would get the same amount of encouragement to do better as Josh would with his B's and C's. The brother and sister ran on different fuel, however, and they each churned their father's strong words into a different end product. For Josh, success at his desk was a necessary pre-requisite for ice time. For Maggie, school success was its own reward.

Setting high standards for grades on their report cards was but one example of John Barber influencing Maggie and Josh to see themselves as capable of being engaged with people in the top tier of any activity. This meant he pushed them in school work and encouraged them to step up and be noticed in any activity. John didn't seek any attention for himself, but he would support the kids to be at the front of the line without any of the typical youngster's fear of the limelight or awe for a "celebrity." "I used to take them to baseball games and concerts, or wherever, and say, 'These people are no different than you. If you want to talk to them, just go talk to them.'"

Josh, in particular, had no fear of going up to people, no matter how famous they were. One Saturday, when he was about eight years old, his older cousin who worked at a restaurant in Newport called the Barber house and said, "Arnold Schwarzenegger and his family are going to be at our restaurant tonight at 6:30 PM. Please don't tell anybody, or I'll get in trouble."

The family didn't have any plans that day, so the four of them got in the car and drove over the bridge to Newport. They parked the car and walked to the area where anyone approaching the restaurant would have to pass. All of a sudden, Josh slipped away from the group and dashed through a narrow alley between two buildings that led to the rear of the restaurant. Moments later, he came back leading Arnold Schwarzenegger and his family.

The sight of their son, who was small for his age, skipping in front of the giant Schwarzenegger, stunned John and Darla. There was a silent moment of suspended action all around as the small boy, the large action-hero/governor, the ordinary parents, and various others looked at one another and absorbed the encounter. And then it was over. John pointed out the restaurant, and everyone began to move again. Josh never revealed what he had said to Arnold, or even if he had spoken at all, but simply led him by the force of a sizeable magnetic personality in a diminutive body.

Some parents might see this type of encounter as mere serendipity, but John cultivated it as a talent in both his children. Through a colleague at work, he had access to two seats at various Red Sox home games. He would alternate taking Maggie and Josh, and they would always go early so that they could watch batting practice and get autographs. One day, John and Josh were on the outfield side of the Red Sox dugout along with a crowd of kids who were all trying to get autographs. Ellis Burks was on the field in front of them, warming up, passing the ball back and forth with another player. John recalls how, in this case, Josh's respectful demeanor won the day. "All the kids were lined up screaming 'Ellis! Ellis!' He was not even acknowledging that they were calling his name. Josh said, 'Mr. Burks,' and he turned right around and came to him and gave him an autograph."

When it was Maggie's turn to go with John to a Red Sox game, she was completely adorable wearing a white Red Sox uniform with the official Red Sox cap over her long blond hair. They arrived early to watch warm-ups as usual. After warm-ups, the players were heading back to the clubhouse for a while before they would fill the dugout. On their way back in, a lot of the players—the stars—would go around and sign autographs for the kids. On this particular day, Wade Boggs came in from third base and started signing autographs right at the backstop. He came around the sweep of the wall to where John and Maggie were waiting, really close to the dugout. Maggie was sitting on top of the wall, very patiently waiting at the end of the line. Boggs made his way around and stopped about ten kids in front of her. He had already turned around and started trotting to the dugout, when he saw her in the uniform. He came back and signed for her.

Wade Boggs was Josh's baseball hero and he was relentless when he learned that his sister had gotten the autograph. "I can't believe she got that autograph! I'm getting one the next time I go." For all his encouragement of the kids, John was thinking, "That's a one-in-a-million shot!" On the way to the next game, Josh had a ball and a pen, and all he could talk about was how he was going to get the autograph. In a complete role reversal, John was cautioning him, "Don't count on it, Josh. I know you want to get your own Wade Boggs autograph, but it's probably not going to happen." But it did. Josh pulled off the magic yet again and surprised his father by getting what he came for. Like Boggs and his hitting streak, Josh just had a knack for swinging and connecting. When Josh had a hero, in sports as a kid, or later in music, it would be nearly a sure thing to bet on his ability to converge and bond with that person.

Wade Boggs' autograph

Being a kid in the pre-teen and early teen years, especially while going through puberty, typically includes episodes of being absent-minded, stubborn, and even downright stupid. Josh was no exception, despite his talent for fun and his focus on the ice. One evening, an hour or so after they had dropped him off at a junior high school dance, his parents got an unexpected call from school officials: Josh was carrying a knife and they had to come and get him. When they arrived at the new Melrose School gymnasium, Josh was standing at the door in his clean white shirt, looking very ashamed. The teacher on duty at the dance reported that he had a small jack-knife and was seen showing it to some other boys. The school's zero tolerance policy for any sort of weapon meant that they had to immediately notify parents and remove the student from school property. Because it was a first offense, no additional punishment followed, but Josh was sufficiently embarrassed by the situation to wish never to bring this kind of attention to himself again. In fact, in talking through the event with his parents, he couldn't even tell them why he had made the decision to bring a knife to school in the first place.

On the cusp of his transition between junior high and high school, Josh took some other risks that are amusing to look back on. At around this time, Darla decided that she could safely leave Josh and Maggie with her mother in order to accompany John on a business trip to Australia. The kids were more accustomed to staying with John's parents; after all, they had lived right next door for years.

Josh was about thirteen and Maggie about ten. They were very capable and mature, but Darla was still nervous about being so far away, and she called the house every day. She sensed almost immediately that the kids and her mom were not getting along too well. As soon as he got on the phone, Josh would blurt out, "Mom, she's driving me crazy."

When Darla asked for specifics, he would say, "She is just driving me nuts! Everything I do is wrong. She says I'm drinking too much milk. I can't do this. I can't do that!"

As a result of so much extra supervision, Josh took initiative on something that was convenient, though perhaps not logical, for his grandmother. He told her that he was allowed to drive his father's little red Toyota truck to take their trash to the transfer station. He must have stated this version of the family routine with great confidence and conviction, because she believed him.

The truck was a standard shift vehicle, and Josh had never driven it by himself. His confidence may have come from an occasion or two sitting on his father's lap steering along a stretch of country road. In between shouts of "I can do it!" and the grinding of gears, they bucked and stalled several miles down North Main Road and accomplished their task. This story, too, has become a family legend, sure to elicit bursts of laughter every time!

John and Darla did not often take advantage of his work travel for their own add-on vacations. Many of their vacations were to visit family in Connecticut or Maine, but there were a number of times when John saved his frequent flier miles and the four of them took a special vacation together. One trip to Hawaii was magical for Maggie and Josh. The Barbers stayed at a resort for over a week, and there were many activities that appealed to kids. One of the resorts had a man-made lagoon with dolphins. Josh and Maggie swam with the dolphins, sometimes holding on to a fin and being pulled through the lagoon. Darla and John took photos of each of them kissing a dolphin on the nose. No one who saw those photos could doubt that these children were loved and treasured and that they were very fortunate to be in a family with so much joy in their healthful amusement.

Moving on to High School

Josh played CLCF hockey through his middle school years, grades six, seven, and eight, becoming a dominant force on the ice and catching the eye of high school scouts. Jamestown doesn't have a high school of its own, but the district has a contract to send students to North Kingstown High School just across the bridge. North Kingstown didn't have a hockey team at the time, so the family faced a huge decision. There were a number of high schools where Josh could play hockey. Three of the best were Portsmouth Abbey in Newport, LaSalle in Providence, and the public high school in the East Greenwich School District. Ben Butterfield was going to Portsmouth Abbey. La Salle had a really outstanding hockey program. East Greenwich had a decent program, but Josh might not be challenged sufficiently there.

John made calls to the coaches at all three schools, and they returned his calls. All three were interested, but at the high school level, it is illegal to recruit student-athletes with scholarships. The Abbey, probably the best of the three schools, stated their full tuition outright with no apologies, but East Greenwich and LaSalle indicated that there were resources that could legally help out with the costs of attending. Josh would have been a star at East Greenwich, but he would be challenged and likely grow as a player in the stronger La Salle program. In addition, one of the Barbers' friends and neighbors in Jamestown was the admissions director at La Salle. His daughter Brooke and Josh had entered kindergarten together, and they were friends all the way through eighth grade. She would be going to La Salle for high school, and perhaps that was the tipping point in the decision. When John thinks back on the deliberations, he remembers the ambivalence. "I really wanted him to go to East Greenwich because he would have been their star right away. Instead, we went with La Salle. I can't really remember why."

La Salle Academy in Providence was the right choice for lots of kids, and in many ways, it was the right choice for Josh. It fielded one of three elite high school hockey programs in New England; everyone in hockey had their eyes on La Salle. For over two years, Josh tolerated hardships so that he could play hockey in an environment where he was matched with his peers, both on his own team and in competition. He was single-minded in this pursuit and shrugged off all other considerations.

Josh's interest in academics slumped at La Salle. He wanted more than the school could offer in art and graphic design and less than they required in religious study. Not one of his academic teachers lit a fire in him for history, languages, literature, or science that could compete with his love for hockey. Off the ice, he never felt the strong sense of really belonging at the school that had been so pervasive through elementary and junior high in Jamestown. To make it all worse, he was beaten and robbed by other students on at least one occasion. Still, he stayed with the whole package, just so he could pursue his passion.

The decision to attend high school at La Salle to play hockey also had a profound effect on Josh's network of friends. After more than eight years of tight relationships within the small Jamestown community, he was virtually cut off from his social network. He was either at school in Providence, at hockey practice or games, or on the road somewhere in between Jamestown and Providence.

Chad Seelig was one of the few Jamestown friends who stayed close to Josh. Their parents had been friends for years, and the boys, who were one year apart in school, had a lot of interests in common. Chad looked up to Josh who was a year older and who seemed very popular and "cool" in the younger boy's eyes. "I've known Josh for almost as long as I can remember . . . maybe even kindergarten. I remember him being a good hockey player, [and] talented artist."

Josh and Chad didn't bond over hockey sticks or paints. They had a natural affinity based on a similar sense of humor, love of adventure, and other interests. As teenagers at different high schools, they re-connected through music.

> One day, Josh showed up with his parents at our house, and we were all talking about music. He was wearing his leather jacket and sun glasses, had long hair, and he was good to talk to. I remember thinking 'He is still a pretty cool kid!' Shortly after that time, we both picked up playing the guitar; he played the electric and I played

the bass. We would jam together in the room over my parents' garage. We would attempt to play Bush, 311, and No Doubt, all popular bands at the time. We had no idea what we were doing but had a great time doing it. He became hooked and had a natural talent; I played for a couple of years and lost interest. At around this same time, we started going to shows together at places like Lupo's and The Strand in Providence. I went to my first concert with him (6/3/96) to hear No Doubt and 311. I still have the ticket.

No Doubt was Josh's favorite band by far. He was obsessed with them! He would study their music, learn every song, and go to meet the band members at autograph signings. He was the ultimate fan. I actually remember him making phone calls to the band members' parents and talking to them about the band and individual band members.

The two boys got into some typical high jinks for kids their age, and all of this would cement the friendship solidly enough to get them through the years of separation in different schools. Josh got his driver's license at least a year before Chad because he was older and also because it was a priority for him to begin driving on his own to keep up with the demanding school and hockey schedule forty miles away. Chad appreciated the adventures proposed by his friend. "Josh had this rear-wheel-drive blue Mercedes that we would take out when there was fresh snow on the roads. We would go out for hours, do donuts in the street, and slide all over the place. Josh was hilarious. He would do these imitations and funny voices. I don't think I have ever laughed so hard as I did then. We had a blast!"

Chad remembers periods of time when they each got busy with school friends and/or girls and wouldn't see each other for months, but eventually they would get together again, and it was always a good time. Josh was a naturally high-spirited, uniquely intelligent, and charismatic person. He was as bold in creating entertaining situations as he was in creating opportunities on the ice. Chad was a lifelong member of his fan club. "Josh would call "The Edge," one of the local radio stations, and do these Sol Rosenberg impressions (character from The Jerky Boys) that were hilarious. They would air him talking to the DJ, a guy named Mad Max. He would call at least once or twice a week, and I would always be listening and trying to tape. He ended up becoming friendly with Max, and I remember meeting him a couple of times with Josh in Providence."

Josh's parents were also big fans of their teenage son's radio performances. John describes an ongoing character skit done entirely in a nasal voice, with an accent imitating the character and skits from The Jerky Boys. The voice Josh adopts is an accident-prone old man obsessed with sex. He calls the radio station to relate his many stunts and to ask Mad Max to play a song for him.

"I've fallen down the stairs and my shoes fell off!"

"I stepped on one of the cats and broke half his ass and now he's going around in circles!"

"I've got a problem over here! I lost my glasses and my eyes are going crazy!"

"Hey! Is this the Mad Hatter? Can you play 'Again' by Alice in Chains for me?"

Josh was so good that sometimes Max would call him and say "I want you to phone me at such and such a time. Call me and we'll put it on the air." Josh would set up the recorder and turn it on to record when the phone rang. The two of them would banter in character for a minute or two over an incident like being stuck in a toilet bowl or the celebration of BJ or VJ day, and then the disc jockey would make a commercial announcement or play a song.

Darla and John loved the radio antics, but they weren't as thrilled when their son was invited to go to bars with Max to do live skits. John said, "Josh was only about sixteen or seventeen, and letting him go to bars with Mad Max always scared me."

Josh was a good kid, and most of his antics were completely harmless. He could be well intentioned and impulsive at the same time, however, and this combination did bring some trouble. Josh was in the lunch room at La Salle one day when he observed a group of kids picking on a particular boy. He watched for a while, but when the kidding and teasing crossed the line to become tormenting, Josh acted. He walked over to the student who seemed to be leading the cruel attacks and dumped his lunch tray over the boy's head.

Back in Jamestown, the phone rang and Darla answered it. The dean of students at La Salle insisted that she immediately come to the school to meet with her and pick up Josh. Darla had already made one trip to La Salle that day, but she got back in the car for the second trip. She arrived and found Josh sitting in the waiting area of the dean's office. He looked completely dejected, with guilt and shame written in his posture and expression. Darla thought he looked like he had already been convicted of a capital crime.

Mother and son went into the dean's office and sat through a severe verbal lashing. Darla was extremely upset by the dean's tone. "She focused on the fact that Josh had made a serious mistake, and that two wrongs don't make a right. In many ways I wanted to agree with her, but her tone was so belittling. She never mentioned the bullying that Josh had witnessed, and she treated him as if he represented the core problem of the whole situation. I felt like she was pummeling Josh unnecessarily."

Josh had never had any particular reason before this to like or dislike the school official, but he really felt hurt by the scolding. His internal moral compass was offended. He knew his own actions were not entirely blameless, but in his mind, a measure of justice had been served. The bully deserved what he had gotten, and Josh withdrew his respect from the official who refused to recognize that.

The whole incident stayed with him. It didn't exactly fester, but he couldn't let it go either. Darla could see that it didn't roll off his shoulders as it might for other kids. When Josh felt mortified, as he did that day, his mother was reminded that her otherwise robust son was hypersensitive in other areas. Still, this didn't color his life on a daily basis; far from it!

After excelling on the junior varsity team for two years, Josh practiced with both JV and varsity teams during the summer after his second year at La Salle. All the sacrifices of the long daily commute to Providence, as well as the shortcomings of his academic experience, would be redeemed by the rewards of being on the varsity team. He worked hard all during that summer to get into tiptop shape and to hone his skills. He felt confident that he was on track to play varsity in the fall. Meanwhile, the school hired a new hockey coach for the varsity team.

The new coach arrived with a plan to build his own team. He had to make room for new players coming into La Salle, so he cut seven of the rising juniors from the team. He announced the names as the players held their breath. One by one, young men who had worked toward a place on this varsity team for years turned away to face a void. The coach said, "Last cut . . ." and Josh knew he was one second away from getting a break or being broken. At the word "Barber," his career in hockey was over.

The shock reverberated far beyond the ice arena. Josh was devastated and bitter. After so many years of thinking of himself as a hockey player, he was, at a stroke, denied that identification. Who was he if he wasn't a hockey player?

Josh's reaction was extreme. He vowed that he would never play hockey again, and furthermore, he was done with all effort and intention related to schools of any kind. His parents had always insisted on grades of at least a B if he wanted to continue playing hockey. That motivation was now gone. He would tolerate the remainder of his high school curriculum and graduate, but he absolutely refused to consider going to college. Darla recalls many heated dinner-table discussions on the topic. No angle or persuasion was effective with the teen who had been abruptly thwarted in his goals. "Josh was just adamant about it. He didn't want to go to college, and we couldn't make him. I finally said 'We're not discussing this at dinner anymore because it is making me sick!'"

Both parents were concerned about how their son would recover from the disappointment that had affected him so deeply and what he would do after graduation. For at least a year after the shock of being cut from the hockey team at La Salle, Josh was much more subdued than the energetic and amusing fellow he had always been. He turned a little more inward but, eventually, he channeled his vast passion for hockey into music.

CHAPTER IV

From Pucks to Picks

The blues is the roots, the rest is the fruits.
Willie Dixon

J OSH WAS SIXTEEN YEARS OLD when his hockey career ended abruptly. This is a vulnerable age for many young people, and he could have diverted all of his energy and commitment from the ice rink to any number of other activities: another sport, girls, drugs and alcohol, video games, cars, etc. He was attracted to drawing and painting but had no access to a dynamic mentor or even to role models. Meanwhile, he had already developed a huge love affair with the rock band No Doubt. In the vacuum left after he was cut from the LaSalle hockey team, Josh began to develop his own musical skills.

Actually, Josh's passion for music started a few years earlier when John took him and his friend Ben Butterfield to a Joe Walsh concert. The boys were about thirteen or fourteen years old, and it was a truly matchless experience, beyond even what John could have planned for, paid for, or predicted. The event was held at an ocean club and it was a completely "standing room only" venue; there were *no* seats. In promoting the show, a local radio station held a "Couch Potato" contest. The winner would get two tickets to sit on a couch placed right in front of the stage. These were not just the best seats but the only seats! Behind the couch was a five-foot high chain link fence to keep the crowd from pressing forward to the stage.

At this time in the early to mid-1980s, Walsh was a big name for his star-quality turns with the James Gang, Barnstorm, and the Eagles, but he was also a sell-out solo performer. John had been a big fan for years, and the young Josh and Ben would soon be inducted into the inner circle of Walsh fandom. This was their first big concert; they were already impressed and keyed up by the high-energy crowd, the setting, and all of the side show attractions. The three of them had arrived early and staked out their territory behind the fence as close as possible to the stage.

Shortly after the concert began, the two fellows who had won the "Couch Potato" contest were feeling a little embarrassed at being in the spotlight, and they turned around and saw John and these two electrified kids. "Hey, this is kind of weird for us," they said to John. "Would you like the kids to come up here instead of us?"

People cheered as John pitched the two excited boys over the fence to take the prized seats on the couch. Joe Walsh was already on stage, and he noticed the switch. He warmed up to the boys immediately and started talking to them over the microphone so everyone could listen in. Josh and Ben gave it right back. Soon, he was throwing them guitar picks and drumsticks. It was like they were part of the show! At one point, Walsh looked directly over to the concession area and demanded, "Bring my friends some drinks!" There was no turning back; this kind of thrill goes right to the bloodstream.

In addition to the imprint of that Joe Walsh concert, Josh had music in his genes and in his experience of extended family and their many gatherings. Darla's sister Candace and her husband Steven had been in a band when they were first married, and they still played guitar and led sing-a-longs at family holiday parties. Her sister Penny and several others also played, and everyone participated when the folk and rock songbooks were brought out.

Perhaps the intense attraction to the musicians of No Doubt was Josh's first independent experience with music. Certainly, Gwen

Stefani alone was enough to draw the attention of a teenage boy! Guitarist Tom Dumont and drummer Adrian Young became two of his early musical role models. Josh even experimented with the outrageous hair styles and outfits of the band. On one occasion, Darla picked up Josh early from his school day at La Salle to take him to meet the band and get Gwen Stefani's autograph. Maggie remembers the infatuation with the band as a time period when she and Josh were close. "Some of the best times that I ever spent with Josh were when we both loved No Doubt. I wasn't driving yet, and I remember thinking as a young teen that it was so cool that I could leave the house without Mom and Dad. Sometimes it was just Josh and me; sometimes my cousin or one of our friends would come along. We both became really intense No Doubt fans and went to numerous concerts together."

When Josh put down his hockey stick and picked up a guitar, he was already steeped in music. The loss of hockey had precipitated a traumatic period, and yet, it could have been so much worse. He channeled the disappointment and hurt into a new passion that would force him to learn new skills and would eventually take him much further and provide even more recognition than had his prowess on the ice.

Like fishing and like ice hockey, once Josh started playing guitar, he was totally committed to it, night and day, one hundred and ten percent! He took that first acoustic guitar and went behind closed doors into his room. He taught himself to play from books and from the Internet. When his musical family members were around, he peppered them with questions and asked for pointers. He roundly refused to take formal guitar lessons for the first couple of years. Mostly he was imitating his No Doubt heroes. He would listen to their songs and then play phrases over and over again until he sounded just like them. This was in the 1990s when Caribbean-inflected "ska" was having a "third wave" of popularity. It wasn't long before he was out of his room and playing short pieces in public.

Josh was still in high school the first time he got on stage to play. The Barbers were in New Hampshire for a holiday with Darla's family, and everyone went out to a local nightclub where Josh's older cousin Shannon worked. They were all sitting around talking, telling family stories, and laughing when Josh took advantage of the band's invitation to get on stage and play a few numbers with them. He didn't sing or even introduce himself. He just got up and tried to fit in with the groove already happening on stage. As he realized people were looking at him and listening to his sound, he gained more confidence and played more openly, aiming his sound to the audience of his family and others in the room. It was impromptu—a surprise to the family and perhaps even to Josh. Still, it marked a turning point. He enjoyed it; he received applause; he saw that he could do more with this new passion.

Just as with hockey, Josh wanted to be improving constantly. He first learned to play by strumming chords, and then he taught himself to pick individual notes and patterns. He didn't read music, but he had an informally trained and eager ear. Having the right instruments and equipment became very important to him very quickly. A typical conversation between Josh and John during his last year of high school would go like this:

"Dad, I need a 'Flying V' guitar because it's the one so-and-so plays in this song."

"Josh, how much money do you have?"

"Dad, can you *please* help me out to buy this guitar? Oh, and by the way, I also have to have a new amplifier because it's the only way I'll get the best tone."

John recognized the gimmicks of advertising and celebrity promotions, but he truly wanted his son to have the right equipment to take his talent as far as he could go. He saw the tiny amplifier that Josh could afford on his own, and he wanted to help.

> One time when we were in Connecticut visiting my family, I happened to pick up the newspaper and spotted an ad for an amplifier. I think it was listed for a hundred bucks. Josh was pretty good by this time and could play the

song, "Riviera Paradise," a difficult instrumental piece. I went to look at the amplifier in some guy's basement. Since I don't play, he was going to demonstrate the equipment. He asked me, 'What kind of music does your son like to play?' I mentioned 'Riviera Paradise,' and he said, 'Oh, I can't play that piece! I only play chords.' I listened to him play and recognized the quality of the equipment. I bought the amplifier, and it was Josh's favorite for many years.

While Josh was learning to play the guitar, he was listening almost exclusively to No Doubt and other hip rock groups in the same mold. His attention was entirely focused, and he had no interest in diversifying. The adolescent Josh refused any offers outside his current interest, and he turned down an invitation to go with his parents to the Newport Blues Festival. There was "no doubt" that music was replacing fishing and hockey as the focal point of Josh's young life. It would, however, evolve for him over time as he matured, and that first refusal would not be his last opportunity to embrace the blues.

Inner Life

The intense personality that his mother recognized in the infant Joshua Adonis back in 1980 had evolved over the years to propel the young man in several areas of life. When he gave himself to fishing, or to hockey, or later to his music, it was with a passionate concentration that drove him toward mastery and innovation; a special sort of intellect. This force has a compelling effect on others. Often, people are drawn to this burning energy because it makes them feel vibrantly alive just by proximity.

Josh entered into relationships with as much passion as he put into his other pursuits. In friendships, family bonds, and romance, he was a most vital partner, seeming to load every experience with more meaning than it ever had without him. For some, he could be like a sort of addiction: life without Josh might seem drab and insipid. With a dose of Josh, life was novel and exhilarating.

Only Josh knew what it felt like to be this charismatic person. It was not a simple thing. His bright lights were accompanied by super-sensitivity and compassion for others. As a toddler, he became distraught when his baby sister cried, and in elementary school, he might burst into tears if he disappointed a teacher's expectation. In adolescence, he was deeply moved and troubled by the plight of a young child with cerebral palsy that Darla was caring for at home during the day. Josh had observed Ashley struggling a number of times at their home. He would return again and again to the question of how there could be a God who would allow this kind of suffering. In his teen years, after having a tooth pulled under sedation, Josh sobbed with deep feelings of empathy for Ashley.

Josh's feelings for Ashley were mutual. A home movie taken when she was only about a year old shows him playing his guitar for her. Darla was there. "Ashley was hooked up to her feeding tube, and Josh was sitting on the couch playing the guitar; she was watching him. The only ways she could communicate were with laughing or crying. She couldn't speak and couldn't do anything for herself physically. But she could relate to him, just as he related to her. Josh was really just taken by her."

The bond with the disabled child Ashley was not unusual for Josh. He didn't pull away or behave awkwardly. He was more likely to approach people and find alternative ways to reach out. Music was one of the ways he did this with a most generous heart, but he would also reach out with his spirit. He connected years later with Rob Goode, a young man who came to hear him play a number of times at the Narragansett Café in Jamestown. Their affinity comes across in a poem the young man wrote: "He plays and sings about things we only dare to think about, refuse or [are] unable to understand." (see Appendix for full poem)

When Maggie talks about her brother, the first comment she is likely to make will be about this intense compassion and empathy for others. "No relationship or interaction in Josh's life is ever shallow. He feels everything to the core, and he processes everything on a very deep level, I think deeper than many people do."

In his journal, Josh opens up a little about what it feels like to be him. He didn't date most of his journal entries.

Ashley
I wish I could take your pain.
Little baby coughs and struggles for every breath of air, we're too stuck in ourselves to even care.
It's easier to ignore.
Where's your god now? The one you speak of the almighty. He does all good, but I guess he let a few slip. For what? Original sin? Fuck original sin. This child was innocent the second it was conceived, yet it's still cursed with problems we can't imagine.
For granted we take our lives and we believe bullshit to make us feel better.

The following journal entry is signed JAB 12/5/98. Josh was eighteen years old when he wrote this meditation following a moment of epiphany that revealed what he felt was the meaning of life. He seems to have very deep concerns about pain, suffering, and death, but the result of his "moment of pure reality" is to reinforce the power of love to overcome all pain and suffering.

Tonight I had "a moment of pure reality" or truth as you may have it. I don't know what caused it particularly, but I know for sure where it came from; deep within me. This is the base of your inner being, your soul. I am not a religious person of sorts, at least not at this point in my life, but tonight I came one small step closer to an answer, to a reality. I cried for what I feel must have been a hidden cut, scrape or burn on my soul. The cry came, as I said, from deep within, and by the time it was over, I felt the need to show all the love that was in me. I reached to my chest to feel my heart beat. It was as though I needed some confirmation I was alive, or some truth about what it meant to be alive. I pondered death for the majority of the cry, as I have before, and much of it dealt with suffering. I flipped past everyone I had come in contact with in my life, friends, family, enemies . . . I heard my father's words several times saying, "you can't cry forever Josh, pretty soon there are no more tears," and I saw him crying from times in the past. And I wondered if he was right. In moments of sheer pain, does there have to be a point where the tears cease . . . or can the pain outlive us? After the cry I had a strong desire to right my wrongs, and in a sense, rid myself of any false tense bullshit, which we all cause for ourselves every waking second of life. I remembered several dreams of the past, from when I was a child to more recent ones. Nightmares dealing with my mother, nightmares of underwater fire . . . recurring daymares you might say, at times when I was supposedly hallucinating from high fevers. I wondered how and why suffering and death exist, and if they could possibly benefit anyone. Now that the crying has stopped, I sit here gathering the thoughts of the past few minutes, and am not sure what I've said so far. I just know that emotions can be the most glorious piece of your life, or the end of life as it exists for you. I intend to enjoy every second of life from here on in, because I know it will not last forever, and will try to let everyone I come in contact with from here on in, know what they mean to me, and how much love I hold inside for all of them. As for the pain and suffering, I still lack a firm grasp on it, as well as death. I'm not sure if I will ever come to a solid conclusion of what it means, but I know there will be more of these "times of pure reality" or "truth" and each one will help me better myself. I can only tell you that love is the strongest thing in life, and it overweighs pain in the end. So keep love in your heart, and it's the best drug for pain you can get.

When he wrote this *moment of reality* journal entry, Josh was a high school graduate working in a pizza joint. He was a novice musician who was starting to explore music beyond his first infatuation. As he gained confidence in his performance abilities and more independence after his high school graduation, he started going to places where he would occasionally be invited onto the stage to jam with other musicians. He expanded his interests through this exposure, and blues gradually became part of his repertoire. In true Josh fashion, once his enthusiasm for the blues was lit, it quickly became a blaze. B.B. King was his new hero, replacing Craig Janney and the musicians of No Doubt. His mother expressed it like this: "Josh could play everything, but the blues was *all* he played. Josh *became* the blues!"

His motivation to learn was strong enough at this point that he sought out a teacher. He didn't want the traditional education of reading music; he was hungry for more and more skills so that he could do what he heard the great blues artists do. He was naturally gifted; he was an unrelenting hard worker, and he was inspired. All three came across in his music. Josh met with Bill Killian in Newport for about six months of lessons. As Killian recalls, "Josh was a special guy on a mission of learning the blues. I encouraged him to go to the blues jam sessions at clubs in Providence."

Becoming a Young Adult

For several years after high school, while he was still learning and incubating his musical talents, Josh worked at Island Pizza in Jamestown. The scars from being surgically cut off the hockey team were obvious when anyone compared him to his friends who were all in college. Josh didn't care. He had been working at Island Pizza part time since high school, and a couple of years later he found himself, at age twenty, doing all the work of a manager and feeling like part of the owner's family. When the business was sold, he stayed with it and became the mainstay of the new owner's team. He was working hard in a responsible position but not earning much. When his parents urged him to think about finding a better job that might lead to a career, he replied that money wasn't important to him.

A year or two later, Josh was changing. He wanted a nicer car and realized that money does matter. It makes a certain style of living possible. At around the same time, the pizza business was up for sale again, and John spoke to Josh about buying it. "I tried to convince him to buy it and run it as his own place. He was still a kid, and he didn't have the money or the credit history to buy it himself. I was going to do it. We were going to do it together. He was kind of into this idea for a while."

John was honest with his son about what owning a restaurant might mean: long hours every day; being in the kitchen or the dining room every evening; being the boss and hiring and firing employees. This was the first time Josh had to confront the big adult question of "What do I want to do with my life?" He could just drift into owning a restaurant because it had been his part time job during high school, or he could deliberately make a change. He gave it serious thought and made a decision. He announced to his family, "I don't want to be at work day and night while my friends are at the beach and having fun. I want to get a regular job where I can earn a good living and go home at five o'clock."

While he was still working pizza, Josh was gaining some notice among local musicians. Before he was of legal drinking age, he had wrangled a fake ID somewhere, and he would hang out at The Call in Providence, hoping for an opportunity to mingle with musicians or play with local blues artists. At least once a week, the musicians would gather for an "open mic" blues jam session. The "jammers" would sign in with their name and instrument. Eventually each one would be called up to play a few tunes with the house band. This kind of venue is a win-win opportunity, attracting aspiring musicians to the bar where they will buy drinks, but also giving them a chance to improve their performance skills in front of other musicians. Darla and John would go along, even though there was no guarantee that Josh would perform, and if he did, what time it might be. They were proud of him each and every time he got up on stage. Jam sessions did not pay anything, and Josh had more ambitious goals. In his journal, he noted the landmark date of his "first paying gig" as 4/28/00. He was twenty years old, and he had earned $60.

Hanging out and occasionally playing at The Call offered Josh more than applause. He met his first serious girlfriend there. Ellen was a bartender at The Call, and they fell in love between blues riffs. Josh would sit at the bar while waiting his turn for a chance in the spotlight, and the two of them would talk. She was older than Josh, and the relationship may have influenced his decision to seek a job with more career potential than Island Pizza.

Josh was also seeking out role models among the professional musicians he met during this period. Tom Ferraro, a seasoned and sought-after guitar player, became more than a role model. At first, Josh was just a twenty-year-old, enthused audience member standing near the stage when Tom played. Josh made a point of showing up at Tom's regular Wednesday night gig and sought him out off stage as well. Casual small talk led to shop talk about guitars and music. Josh would persistently badger the more experienced musician for his advice on equipment. Ferraro saw something of his younger self in Josh. They became friends. Tom recalls, "I had been performing for over a decade when I met Josh. He was still a kid. That's what we called him, 'The Kid.' He had a bit of a cocky, know-it-all attitude, but when I got to know him, I realized it was mostly bravado."

The friendship would not have happened if Josh didn't have talent, yet it was not a case of discovering the next blues giant. Compared with the professionals, Ferraro felt his playing was flawed, but in the field of those showing up for jams, he was markedly better than most. "He had a more mature approach compared to the other guitarists who showed up," according to Ferraro. "Josh did not play a lot of notes, and that is a hallmark of someone who can play good blues."

Tom Ferraro already had many years as a musician in his kit when Josh met him. He had played blues or blues-based music in clubs throughout New England but also a number of gigs elsewhere across the United States. He had been part of several recordings and had played or written songs with national releases by other artists. He, too, had heroes of great blues artists and had worked with some of them: Hubert Sumlin, Pinetop Perkins, Joe Beard, Eddie Kirkland, and Mitch Woods. When Tom Ferraro heard Josh play, it was with an ear steeped in tradition and consistently disciplined craft. "To be honest, I was not overly impressed. I could hear his influences and could pick out some faults which I would attribute to lack of stage experience. He was only nineteen or maybe twenty at the time and this is common."

Tom Ferraro knew a whole lot about music and the blues that Josh didn't know. He knew that the public could not distinguish a mediocre guitar player from a really good guitar player and that it is really difficult to improve from being mediocre to being good. "The public is clueless about who is a good musician. They listen with their eyes, and if you're flashy, people think you're good."

Mentoring his eager young friend was effortless for Ferraro. He had been through the tough life decisions and various stages of maturity and professionalism as a musician that Josh would face over the next couple of years. He had seen plenty of young musicians crash and burn and could speak from experience when Josh seemed uncertain and also when he seemed overly determined to pursue a particular strategy. "Josh drove me nuts with his obsession over equipment! He was always talking about buying another guitar or amplifier. I used to tell him, 'It's not about the guitar, Josh. There's no magic bullet for break-through success.'"

With his personal persistence, a measure of talent, and the friendship of an honest and experienced musician, Josh had ahead of him a great opportunity for an education. In other areas of his life, similar developments were occurring.

Having a mentor in his music life, combined with the commitment to leave the pizza business and get a "real job," meant that Josh had become an adult. John encouraged him to apply for a position at the McLaughlin Research Company (MRC), a contractor for the

Naval Undersea Warfare group. He was offered a job working in the graphics department, and he entered the facility as an employee for the first time on June 6, 1999. Josh had a lot of talent in this area, and his colleagues at MRC embraced this capacity, giving him many complex projects.

John tells a story about Josh's early skills in this area emerging when he was only ten years old. This was in 1990, and the Barbers had an old Macintosh computer that Josh was far more proficient on than either of his parents. Those early machines came with a drawing program called MacPaint, and Josh had taught himself how to use it.

> We had been on vacation in Hawaii when a building blew up at the Naval Base. I had to go into work the Sunday we returned and work seven days a week, many hours a day, for a long period. We were conducting an investigation, just like the NTSB does after a plane crash, trying to recreate what happened so that it would never happen again.

> Some of the experts on this investigation weren't familiar with the system that had detonated, so I was constantly at a whiteboard drawing all the systems, all the piping, components, and everything. One day my boss said to me, 'We should have that diagram to pass out so you don't have to draw it over and over.' I went home and gave it to Josh. He took my hand-drawn sketches and made an accurate graphic on the Mac and we began to use it. It has since been revised and upgraded a few times, and it's now part of official documentation for the Navy.

When he was a teenager, Josh had also designed several logos for international user conferences that his father conducted for representatives of all the countries that use a particular weapon crafted by the U.S. Navy. He loved graphic design and had a substantial portfolio of work even before his first day on the job at MRC. His ultimate success in the department—or possibly his talents at the "drawing board"—might have been a handicap, however. After about a year, Josh began to feel that he couldn't advance anywhere in this group, so he transferred out of graphics and into a division called the "shapes lab."

In addition to supporting the Naval Undersea Warfare Center with graphics, MRC also runs a program to test mock-up torpedoes. These replicas don't contain explosives. MRC personnel take an existing torpedo, do any necessary maintenance, mount it in a submarine, shoot it, bring it back, and do maintenance again. They are testing for all of the performance characteristics except for explosive functions. It is a very hands-on, mechanical job. MRC is located in the industrial park in Middletown, Rhode Island, but the torpedo testing happens at the NUWC in Newport. In this role as a torpedo technician, Josh would find himself working at the same facility where his father worked, often with the same people.

Josh worked at MRC for nearly nine years, more than half of that time with torpedoes. Even though he had shifted away from his love of graphic design, he enjoyed the charged atmosphere of working on-site at the Undersea Warfare Center. He had worked on car engines with John as a teenager and was comfortable around tools, machine parts, and power equipment. He had the patience to detect and correct small defects, and his skills did not go unnoticed. He was recognized for his achievements, and there was always real potential for career advancement ahead of him. At the same time, this job was secondary to Josh; it did not excite his passion or inspire him. He would complain to friends that he didn't really like his work. He was fulfilling his craving for intensity in his alternative life as a blues musician outside of work hours.

During the same years that Josh worked at MRC, he built an after-hours career of some renown. It started with several years of regularly stepping into jam sessions at various clubs in Rhode Island.

Josh had a particular genius for connecting with people, and even the best known performers soon acknowledged him by name for his unique musical style. Just like the little boy who would get the coveted autograph, Josh was able to assert his forceful energy to meet and mobilize to his cause the people he would need as a musician. As he became more and more familiar with the scene, he started to believe that he could succeed at another level. He advertised for musicians to join him in a band he called Smokestack Lightnin'.

The key to the group's charisma for the following seven years would be Josh's talent and drive, along with Nino Paldan's vocal gifts and greater experience. Nino had moved to the United States from Sweden where he had been in a very popular band. He was older than Josh and very comfortable with the spotlight, whether he was singing, playing harmonica, or just introducing a new song. His strong voice and superb playing were key for the new group. The two of them formed the core, and other musicians would follow their lead. The original band was Josh, Nino, Chad Sousa on drums, and Chad's father, Dick Sousa, on bass. Over time, many people filled the positions around Josh and Nino, but the two of them really made the music happen. Josh networked and booked the gigs, and Nino held the group to a disciplined standard that paid high dividends. Smokestack Lightnin' was named "Best Rhythm and Blues Band in Rhode Island" in both 2004 and 2008.

The years 2000 to 2005 were good years. Josh had a job with excellent career potential, and his music provided the zest of fresh challenges and rave reviews. He had moved out of his parents' home and was living with his friend Chad in a great house right on the water. The relationship with Ellen was steady and strong despite their increasingly different views of their future as a couple.

Chad Seelig, Josh's good friend since grade school, had been a music partner early on, and they remained friends over the years. Josh was a couple of years out of high school, working full time and playing music when Chad was just starting college. Josh found he could enjoy the very best parts of college by hanging out with Chad and his roommates on weekends. According to Chad, Josh was part of many a movie-worthy scene.

> The partying, the girls, I mean how could you go wrong? There was this place on campus called DP Dough that was known for their calzones. They delivered all night, and Josh would typically order two Hawaiian calzones for himself, after asking everyone else what they wanted to order. He was willing to pay for theirs because he wanted those two Hawaiians all to himself. No one had any money in college, so they would say no, and then mooch off him. Despite his warnings, he would always share. One night, my roommate asked Josh for a bite of the calzone. Josh tossed him the box, and it opened in midair. A cup of marinara sauce spilled all over my roommate and the couch. My roommate wasn't too happy, but Josh and I were rolling on the ground in tears from laughing so hard. Everyone liked Josh; he was friendly, funny, and entertaining.

In the summer of 2003, the two young men lived together in a Jamestown rental on the water. They continued to enjoy the college party life, with success measured in the number of kegs consumed. It was not unusual for the crowd to polish off four kegs. Their flip cup games were massive, with twenty players on each team.

Late at night, Chad reports, "Josh would break out the guitar and play for everyone. People would go nuts because he was so good at it. Play behind his head, play these crazy solos. This stuff that you would only see in a music video. It was really cool. It felt like we were in those movies where the parents leave for the weekend, and the kids throw this huge party that everyone talks about."

Even when the two of them were alone in the house, that summer was magical. Over the following year or two, they were still close friends, and Chad would recruit twenty or more friends to go to any venue where Josh and Smokestack Lightnin' were playing.

Growing Pains

Every family goes through several transitions; one of the most dramatic is when children leave home, and relationships must be renegotiated on new terms. The Barber family was first and foremost a tightly-knit unit. No matter where their lives took individual members, they gathered for dinner regularly and kept in close touch. Even when they didn't talk every day, each of them knew that, at a moment's notice, a cohort of support could be summoned, without question, day or night, rain or shine. Within this context, family bonds were flexible and could even stretch thin at times.

Josh had mixed emotions when Maggie graduated from high school and went off to college at the University of Rhode Island. He loved and was proud of his little sister. She had been such a good buddy, keeping up with the bigger kids and tagging along to so many hockey games. She had been an eager companion to enjoy the music he loved, and she was tremendously proud of his success with Smokestack Lightnin'. Here she was, three years younger, however, going off to college, beginning to live her own life separate from the family and from him. He had made different choices, and even though he felt secure with those choices, watching Maggie's young adult life take a turn away from his chosen path did send a few shockwaves his way. His life at high school commencement had not seemed as simple and clear as Maggie's looked to him now.

As Maggie recalls, she and Josh were not as close during the five years she lived away from home for college and beyond. At times, she was even glad to have the escape of "going home" to her apartment after a family dinner. There was a particular pattern to their interactions that she hadn't recognized before but that was less and less comfortable to her as she grew into her own adulthood. Maggie was gravitating toward courses in counseling, psychology, and sociology. She found herself more interested in questions of motives, intentions, and consequences, rather than in absolutes of good and bad, right and wrong. Josh was resistant to Maggie's new ways of thinking and discussing issues. Perhaps she was just not agreeing with him as much as before, but he found himself telling her, quite often and quite vigorously, that she was wrong. "You're wrong! Why would you try to sugarcoat the issue and smooth it over? It is what it is! Let's just look at it in black and white and not fuss about all this warm and fuzzy stuff!"

Maggie called Josh's tone "blunt," and his father sometimes referred to him as "grumpy." "He was a little grumpy with people that he was close to. It's much easier to be grumpy with your family and close friends. But with other people that he wasn't close to? He was completely charismatic." Some people saw both sides of Josh and accepted that he could sometimes seem like a person with two contradictory ways of behaving. He could be charming and vibrant on one occasion, and scowling and irritable on another. The contradictions extended to his feelings about his own achievements. He was successful, but not happy, with his work, and he was not satisfied with his music and was constantly challenging himself to achieve more.

The Ups and Downs of Love

Josh was pretty seriously involved with Ellen in 2002 and 2003. Darla and John watched the relationship develop and thought the two of them were a good match. Josh brought her into the family as he always did with his friends. She went with him to visit Yia Yia in Florida after Poppy died. The two of them took Yia Yia to a B.B. King concert, her first but not her last!

Josh and Ellen were together through enough emotional turbulence to feel the strength of their bond. She was part of a significant rite of passage with both Josh and Maggie. In February, 2003, Josh was still living with Chad in the rented house on Seaside Avenue in Jamestown. When he moved there, he took his childhood dog Skilo to live with him. Skilo had been like another sibling to both Josh and Maggie, but now she was old and failing. For all his experience pulling live fish out of the ocean and watching them die, Josh had little experience with warm-blooded death. He was confident that Skilo would always be there to greet him when he got home from work. One day, he walked into the house and she didn't appear. She was dead.

Josh needed to tell the story over and over of how he found her, and Maggie and Ellen listened. "She suffered all day long. There was a trail of blood and shit all through the house! A long message of suffering. I should have been there with her!" Josh had followed the trail and found the dog's slightly warm body. It would have been a shocking and horrific scene for anyone, but for Josh, with his finely attuned empathy, it was more than traumatic.

He cleaned up the bloody mess before he called and told Maggie that Skilo had died. John and Darla were out of town at the time, so it was rather a huge experience for the two siblings to figure out how to deal with this without their parents who typically guided and supported them through everything. Ellen was there with them through all of it.

Josh decided that they must bury Skilo in Jamestown on the property at their parents' home. It was winter and the ground was frozen solid. Josh dug a hole in the back yard entirely by himself. Josh, Ellen, and Maggie were all crying as they placed Skilo in the hole and covered her up. Just a few days later, dozens of young people just their age died in a fire at The Station nightclub not far away. The ache of losing a family pet was always linked in those three hearts with that overwhelming tragedy.

Ellen was with Josh for many more joyful family occasions. She attended at least one of the Barber family's famous Father's Day picnics with extended family at Beavertail. The two of them seemed very happy together for a couple of years, but eventually the difference in their ages became an issue. Ellen was older than Josh, and she was ready to settle down and have a family. Josh was not. He was young and just beginning to feel the powerful draw of success with his music. Darla and Maggie were sure that he really loved Ellen; it just wasn't the right timing for the two of them.

In his journal, Josh tried to cope with the indecision and then the pain by putting it on the page.

> *Night comes and the day ends.*
> *After 2 years, we come close to an end.*
> *. . .*
> *Such a hard choice.*
> *Should I stay or should I go?*
> *Or should I stay and still go?*
> *I'm so afraid to waste your*
> *Precious time More so than mine.*
> *Yeah, I've got a little more time*
> *To work with. Two loves,*
> *You . . . and music.*
> *Root problems*
> *I loathe my 9-5*
> *And I'm not a musician yet.*
> *What to do. How to fix it?*
> *I appreciate your patience more*
> *Than you know.*
> *. . .*
> *I love you. I love music.*
> *Do I need to choose one or the other?*

There was no easy way to blame either of them when the relationship came to an end. Josh knew it wasn't going to work out, and it felt like a body-blow when they finally stopped seeing one another. It was hard for him in so many ways, some of which were profound and inexpressible. For several days after the final breakup, he cried for hours and had difficulty moving away from the sense of a huge loss in his life. Finally, in his journal, he reported a "spot of relief" that they were both turning toward a new chapter in their lives.

5/22/04

Ellen—

So now it's over. Official. Papers signed.

Are you changing your mind? Don't make

It harder than it already is. It's over.

We love each other and always will,

But must not be 'in love' with each other.

If we were I wouldn't feel a

Spot of relief amongst the pain.

I'm sorry if I held you back.

The "spot of relief" expanded gradually, and Josh was able to see that his future without Ellen could be just as happy. When Josh loved someone, it was with his whole being, and the breakup with Ellen was dreadful for him. While in the middle of it, he had a hard time seeing beyond the pain. With the support of family and friends, he managed to keep his focus on work and his music. It was a dark night, but it passed. Josh had a vibrant personality, and of course, there would be other relationships. He eventually started dating again.

CHAPTER V

Evolution

I merely took the energy it takes to pout and wrote some blues.
Duke Ellington

ALONG WITH HIS DEEPENING COMMITMENT to the blues, Josh had adopted a new set of heroes. For starters, he idolized Stevie Ray Vaughan, and he soon began to model his own style on that of Doyle Bramhall II. He occasionally made trips to Austin, Texas, to get into jam sessions with Bramhall and others who had become well-known in blues circles. The jam sessions led to more personal relationships. John and Darla realized that their son was plugged into the main line of the blues one day when they were riding along with him in his car. Josh answered a call on his cell phone and after the conversation, they asked who he was talking to.

"That was Doyle Bramhall."

"Why is he calling you?" Darla asked, surprised.

"We're friends. I see him when I go to Austin, and we like playing together."

Josh was thrilled to be meeting musicians in Austin from 2004 onward: Kim Wilson, Nick Curran, Troy Gonyea, Derek Trucks, Susan Tedeschi, Doyle Bramhall II, Jimmie Vaughan, Preston Hubbard, Lou Ann Barton, and others. He was drawn to the performers and the scene at Antone's, a well-known blues nightclub.

Just like his encounters with Wade Boggs, Arnold Schwarzenegger, and Jim Carrey, Josh was comfortable stepping up to smile for photos with his heroes. He would act like they were his friends, and soon enough, it was true.

Being a friend in the music business is a flexible affair, especially when two parties are not peers in the sense of their reputation and following. It can be a complex mix of affinity, apprenticeship, favors, and competition. One of the true models of friendship in Josh's music life was his relationship with Tom Ferraro. Tom wanted Josh to succeed to the full extent of his talent and his desire. In his view, even talent wasn't a guarantee of success. The formula also included a lot of hard work and hustling on the business end of things, single-minded purpose, focused development of style and skills, good timing with trends in music, and the two unpredictable factors of the generosity of others and good old-fashioned luck. Through his twenties, Josh was experimenting with all of these variables like a sound engineer at a mixing console, sliding the marker up or down on each element to optimize the mix.

Despite his own successful career as a musician, Tom Ferraro always had a day job. Even if they didn't have long discussions about this choice, Josh could see what made up the balance of this successful musician's life.

Josh had the talent—and the equipment—to be recognized as an up-and-coming blues guitarist. Older musicians saw his potential, but they saw some of the rough edges as well. His taste for electric blues heading into rock and roll always produced standout performances, but these would not play to sell-out crowds. His generation was headed in a different direction.

Getting closer to Josh meant that Tom Ferraro noticed patterns that a casual observer might miss. Josh was drinking more than was good for his music. "One time he came over to my house, and I asked him if he wanted anything to drink. He replied, 'Yeah . . . a shot of Crown Royal.' I gave him what I had instead, and after he took the shot from me, he said he thought he may have a problem with alcohol and drugs. I stood up and grabbed the glass from him and chewed him out. Josh was very stubborn at times and not only knew all the answers but the questions too. We talked about going to an AA meeting, but he didn't want to. From then on, when he came over, I limited him to one drink, and I would tell him that he was headed nowhere fast if he kept this up."

A few years later, this was still an issue. Tom felt that Josh was drinking more and more and that sometimes he was drunk by the end of his gigs. His playing suffered for it. Again they had talks about his drinking.

There were times when Josh contemplated a complete break with family, friends, work, and all of his past life to start over in Austin, Texas, as a full-time musician. Because he knew Josh across several years and phases of maturation as a performer, Tom Ferraro could see and understand the extent of Josh's desire for this kind of dramatic change. "He wanted the full bore musician's life and he wanted to be a star, but not quite as much as he let on. It was important to him, but not as important as a couple of other things in life. I believe having a family was ultimately the most important goal on his list. Working hard for that top level of success in music was a struggle he never really embraced."

Ferraro encouraged the younger man to get an education. Josh had told him that his father had offered to pay for any college of his choice but that he didn't want to go to school. He was a little more open to taking guitar lessons, and so his friend found him a teacher. "I set him up with an excellent jazz guitarist who could help him understand theory and become a better player. The lessons were a flop. He took one or two and never went back."

Despite turning away from both college and musical training, Josh was growing in hands-on practical experience of how the world works. He began to see how many friendships in the music business were based on people seeking help and advantages. He learned how to promote his band and get gigs, even when it meant that he was antagonizing others in the business. His friend saw this, but in some ways, it was all part of the road to success. "Josh was very determined to get work and could be a bit abrasive with club owners. You could take this as arrogance, but to his credit, he did get the band working. It was very important to him to be taken seriously. Did he burn bridges? Yes. Did he piss people off? Yes. Was he arrogant? Yes. But Josh was never cold and calculating or malicious. He wanted his fifteen minutes of fame, and he did everything he could to push the band."

Tom Ferraro was a father-figure to Josh in the music business. He wouldn't flinch when honest feedback was called for about Josh's style on stage or off. He could credit Josh with maturity, generosity, and fairness and still recognize the rough edges that came across when he would hustle gigs and special favors. Ferraro tried to instill professional discipline while giving Josh opportunities and advice. He called Josh to the stage, invited him into the recording studio, and welcomed him into his home. The lesson on any given day or night might be about musical protocol, guitar technique, substance abuse, work/music balance, or life in general.

All of this mentoring and education out of school led to more assured leadership of Smokestack Lightnin'. After he connected with blues artists in Austin on several trips, Josh didn't second-guess so often his choice of music, his approach to a classic tune, or his tendency to improvise. He became less deferential to Nino. For the first several years of their partnership, Josh was in the background when the band was on stage. The spotlight would be on Nino singing in the front. Josh was the lead guitar player, but he tended to stay in the shadows. Darla would try to wave him over into the lights. "As parents we would be gesturing and saying to him, 'move over so we can see you!' I think he was still a little shy and nervous on stage."

Despite his own feelings about being in the limelight, Josh knew how important it was to a young musician just getting started. Up to now, Josh had been on the receiving end of notice by many more well-known musicians. He had loved being called to the stage by name-brand performers who recognized his talents. One night in late June of 2007, Josh would pay it forward for a very young and talented guitar player.

Mike Roberts was about fifteen years old, and he reminded Josh of himself at around that age. Mike was a passionate musician, and he was fearless in seeking out the people who would become his mentors and role models. Mike and his father were driving up to Rhode Island from New York for the Jimmie Vaughan show in Providence, and meeting Josh was high on Mike's agenda. He had discovered and contacted Josh through YouTube, and this weekend would be the first of several times that Josh invited Mike on stage to play with him. On the night after the Jimmie Vaughan concert, Josh and the band were playing at Okie's in Narragansett, and Mike and his dad would be in the audience. The young man was thrilled to step up and play his first riffs for the crowd.

Josh was about ten years older and beyond Mike musically, just far enough in the lead to be a mentor but also not so far ahead as to make the achievement seem impossible. They formed a strong bond that continued on and off for a number of years. Mike credits Josh for encouraging and teaching him. "I would not be where I am today without him. He got me started musically, motivated me, taught me, he was my 'dad' of music . . . We were quite close at one point, talking every day . . . [he was] giving me tips and advice on guitars, blues, music, everything. Josh played a major part in the beginnings of my musical career."

Mike Roberts went on to study at Berklee College of Music in Boston. Even then, as a serious student of music, a short text message from Josh—"caught a video of you and your band on youtube, you sound great kid, keep on goin!"—would put a great big smile on his face. The feeling was mutual. Josh trusted Mike to appreciate the energy and devotion that goes into making music. They could talk about the great Doyle Bramhall and be understood. When Josh shared with Mike that he was thinking of selling the guitar he had purchased from Bramhall, Mike felt that there was some significance to Josh's letting go of something that had always been so precious to him.

Blues and Then More Blues

After years of success together, a transition was brewing for Josh in the evolution of Smokestack Lightnin'. Nino Paldan was just the right man at the right time to launch the band with Josh, but as they played together for years, their different styles and habits rose more and more to the surface and caused friction between them. Their success was built upon a foundation of Josh's hustling and networking to get gigs, Nino's disciplined rehearsal standards, Josh's fabulous guitar stylings, and Nino's robust singing and harmonica playing. This advantageous collaboration carried them to award-winning heights for a number of years, but their basic personalities were different.

One of Josh's most audience-pleasing moves was playing the guitar behind his head. He would lift it up and play it in the air behind him with just as much dexterity as he did holding the guitar in front. And the crowd would go nuts. Nino didn't especially like that sort of flashy trick. Nino had a pure blues sensibility. He did not naturally invite rock and roll into their repertoire, nor did he favor including pop tunes or any fusion of these styles. He held to a traditional, old time blues songbook. This was certainly their strong suit, but it became a constant strain on Josh, who wanted to cut loose from time to time. In addition, as the guy booking their schedule, Josh was hearing from clubs that their patrons wanted to dance.

Josh realized that he couldn't continue to get gigs without making some changes. To keep the group alive, he would have to take more control. He asserted himself and told Nino, "*This* is what we'll be playing from now on."

Nino agreed reluctantly and stayed with the group for a while longer, but from that point onward, there was some friction between the two of them. Josh started playing with pedals and experimenting with different sounds. John's impression was that during this transition, "the music got a little louder than ever before." Josh felt the audience loved it. Nino did not.

It was a rocky transition internally, but Josh presented it on his Web site as a positive transformation.

> *As a departure from the original Smokestack Lightnin' which was still going strong although stale within, Josh started to take on more of his own sound/style of playing rather than the straight ahead West Coast Swing and downer blues they revolved their sets around. He started to develop his own vocals and songwriting as well, calling the all new lineup what it's known as today; JB & The Stack or commonly shortened to The Stack.*

The sidemen of The Stack were a steady core of three or four musicians with regular subs, but the band was different from Smokestack Lightnin' in several ways. Josh was now the headliner and star performer. The disciplined rehearsals that Nino had orchestrated were gone. Josh would play all of the main parts and the others would support him and fill in musically. They were still sought after and extremely popular, but it was a different experience entirely.

In his quiet, private moments, Josh had yet another musical persona that was rarely revealed. He wrote subdued songs that he would accompany on his acoustic guitar and record on his equipment at home. A family member or friend might see him sitting alone on the couch or out on the deck. He might be singing to himself in a soft voice, almost silently, testing the sound just barely outside his head.

Seeking a particular sound or effect, Josh would buy a guitar, play it for a year or two, and then decide whether to sell it or keep it. He sometimes owned five or six at a time. Over the years, he probably owned twenty or more guitars, which is not unusual for a musician. Of course, he had to have one of each type of guitar delivering certain tones.

When Darla Barber asserted that "Josh became the blues," she was pointing, perhaps unconsciously, to a whole worldview reflected in a musical style. On his Web site, Josh explained his musical evolution.

> *Growing up he [Josh] listened to little more than classic rock from his father's collection and radio. Names like Led Zepplin, Dire Straits, Jethro Tull, Pink Floyd, Joe Walsh, Cream, Blind Faith, Peter Frampton, and Queen, just to name a few. Josh notes the first live show he ever attended was Joe Walsh with his dad. He claims he grew tired of playing "air guitar" at some point and asked for his first guitar. But he was getting into ska-influenced rock bands like No Doubt, and Goldfinger at the late age of 16 when he first picked it up. He bashfully admits to driving his family nuts playing the opening riff of No Doubts', Just A Girl on his bottom of line Epiphone electric; day in and day out until he started to learn other tunes, but it was the day he was first formally introduced to The Blues, that EVERYTHING changed. The music meant something. It was alive. He actually felt what he played inside, technique took a backseat, and tone and feeling became all that mattered.*

Josh was answering the call of a compelling musical genre. In his classic book, *Stomping the Blues*, Albert Murray writes about some of the misconceptions that revolve around the music called the blues: "Blues music . . . is neither negative nor sentimental," according to Murray. It is not a form of therapy, nor is it a whining complaint set to music, as some have assumed. Rather, the blues takes a kind of heroic stance that extends beyond the music into a perspective on how to live a life. Murray offers a definition.

> [The blues] is a statement about confronting the complexities inherent in the human situation and about improvising or experimenting or riffing or otherwise

playing with (or even gambling with) such possibilities as are also inherent in the obstacles, the disjunctures, and the jeopardy. It is also a statement about perseverance and about resilience and thus also about the maintenance of equilibrium despite precarious circumstances and about achieving elegance in the very process of coping.

Even before embarking on full adulthood, Josh had felt the heavy hand of disappointed hopes. Through no fault of his own, he had been rejected at the very moment he was expecting to be rewarded with an opportunity to deploy and develop his skills in the limelight of varsity hockey. He had also felt the full force of romantic love and loss. These are the ups and downs of ordinary life. The music, lyrics, and beat called "the blues" is what Murray labels a "counteragent" that enables people to acknowledge and overcome inevitable struggles by means of "the dance-oriented good-time music also known as the blues." Through his music, Josh could work through the struggles of life with equally strong impulses toward self-expression and transformation. Throughout the music's long history beginning with African-American work songs, it captured the lows of human existence along with vibrant survival instincts and intense self-awareness.

Anyone watching Josh articulate the blues through his guitar could see, hear, and feel that this music was a language, a creative channel, and much more for this young man. With heart-stopping technical skill and a range from dusky and low-down to penetrating and exuberant, Josh produced a current of life force strong enough to transport forty or fifty people out of their seats all at once. To each person listening, the lyrics and sound might convey something slightly different—longing, regret, defiance, inspiration, resignation, doubt—and for Josh, it was all of these.

From the time he was a baby, Josh had always been a conduit for intense feelings, and this trait powered his appeal as a performer who could tap into the emotions of an audience. He could bear witness to human suffering, both individual and collective, through lyrics and still express affirmation and hope through the sinew and vitality of compelling and unique sound patterns based on a rich history. His own doubts and fears were alive in the music. He was finger-picking hope, fortitude, patience, and a measure of joy as he played. He played the blues to bring all of this to others but also to persuasively fill his own life with meaning and reward.

Complete Happiness?

Josh brought to his music—and to his friendships and romantic relationships—an intensely empathetic spirit. He was aware of other people in a way that couldn't help being attractive. A young, good-looking man playing electric blues might be a magnet to women in all cases, but Josh had also been a magnet from childhood with his vibrant, full-of-fun way of approaching life. He never had trouble making friends or attracting girls. Maggie, one might say, was the first girl who fell head over heels for him. As a big brother—three years older—Josh was her idol and her best friend. And he was not the typical prankster older sibling. In his shoes, another boy might push his little sister aside for guy friends and girls his own age, but most of the time, Josh included Maggie as a welcome part of his social life.

All through his life, in addition to romantic relationships, Josh also had close female friends. Kristy Arnold was an adventure pal for both kids growing up, and he had a most comforting and close friendship with Melissa Ceprano at that late-twenties stage of life when both were contemplating forming new families. Brooke Aldrich and Josh were friends all through school. They started kindergarten together, and it was her father who suggested that Josh apply to La Salle for high school so that he could play competitive hockey. Brooke was truly the only friend from elementary and junior high in Jamestown who went to high school with Josh. They went to at least one prom together, but they were mostly just good pals. He dated a few girls during high school, but the family didn't get to know them because they lived quite far away. Josh's relationship with Ellen was his first real adult relationship, and it was most sincere and passionate.

The texture of romantic relationships changed as social networking matured along with the generation coming into adulthood in the first decade of the twenty-first century. It wasn't long before they were seamlessly entwined. Josh was an early adopter and energetic user. At first, he talked about every connection, new friend, news about old friends, and so on with Maggie and his parents. The Internet was a nifty way to get in touch and plan activities. Eventually, his online relationships formed a separate world, parallel to the flesh and blood life, and he didn't report so much about the relationships there because they were so prolific and intricate.

Josh met a girl on MySpace in 2005. At this time, MySpace was just about at the top of the heap of social networking sites. It seemed to be all good; no one saw any downside to this amazing new toy. That's what it felt like, a great toy that young adults could play with, making friends, posting what they were doing, peeking into other people's lives. Early on, it all felt so harmless. Years later, it would become apparent that, human nature being what it is, technologically augmented relationships magnified human traits, both positive traits and those that could become more harmful when amplified.

Some commentators would even argue that few, if any, positive traits are encouraged by the medium. Computer scientist Jaron Lanier writes in his 2010 book, *You Are Not a Gadget: A Manifesto*, that "The most important thing about a technology is how it changes people . . . A new generation has come of age with a reduced expectation of what a person can be, and of who each person might become." The creation of an identity on a social media site conforms to the design of the site rather than to the unique traits and circumstances of the individual. If there is no check box for your particular situation, you must check an existing box and reduce the "weirdness"—as Lanier puts it—of who you really are. How long does it take, when a particular site is broadly used, for the individual to begin living as though he or she conformed to all the check boxes? Lanier holds that it is an "illusion that digital representations can capture much about actual human relationships."

After some weeks of a developing friendship online, Josh and Angela decided to connect in person, and Maggie happened to be there to meet her that very first time. John and Darla were away on a trip, and Josh had invited Angela to meet him in Jamestown, where both young Barbers were living. It was summer and Maggie had been out somewhere with her friends. When she came home that evening, she could hear Josh talking with a girl out on the deck. She went out to see who it was, and Josh introduced her to Angela.

Maggie felt the spark between them, although Josh kept denying there was anything romantic going on. "They both seemed almost giddy with delight at being together. They couldn't stop talking, jumping from topic to topic like they had to catch up on years of important news."

Maggie noted that there was no touching between them. Josh insisted for a long time that they were just buddies, but Maggie wasn't buying it. Hanging out with them for a little while on the deck convinced her that it was the beginning of more than just a buddy-buddy friendship. She sensed that light and joyful feeling surrounding the honeymoon phase of a romantic relationship, when just everything is so new and so enchanting.

Josh's parents first met Angela several weeks later when she came to Okie's Bar in Narragansett to hear him play. John and Darla were loyal groupies; they went to every performance, anywhere in Rhode Island. Josh had told them that Angela was going to be there, so they felt that this night would be different. "She is just someone I met on MySpace, just a friend. She's pretty cool, but we're not involved. She just wanted to come hear me play." Josh went on for a bit longer than seemed necessary for merely meeting a buddy. It was a very cordial meeting; their common interest—Josh—was in the spotlight and everyone was as animated as the music.

"Have you seen Josh play before?" John asked Angela. "No, this will be the first time." she replied.

Angela was, that night and for a long time afterwards, Josh's most enthused fan. He was on stage all night but made a point of coming over to chat with them during breaks. According to John, "Angela was as cute as a button," and he could sense his son's fascination with her. He didn't for one minute believe that these two were going to remain just buddies for long.

Everyone brings along into a new relationship all of their past experiences and accessories. Sometimes these are obvious and sometimes not. Angela came to the relationship with two children. At first, Josh just ignored this fact; he was simply captivated with the person in front of him, Angela. Within a couple of months, they were both feeling a connection much deeper than the first romantic rush, and that's when her two young sons entered the picture. Jason and Nicholas soon became integral to the relationship between Josh and Angela. The four of them became a family.

John knew that Josh had some hesitations about suddenly taking on the role of a father-figure to these children. The two of them had several discussions about it. John questioned Josh. "What are you going to do when you realize that you are in love with her? It'll be too late to make any decisions. If you want a decision like you are talking about, you've got to make it now."

"No, no. We won't ever get that serious."

Darla's perspective was a bit different, and time proved her to be right. "Josh fell in love with this girl and her two adorable little boys. He loved them like they were his own, as did we. They were going to have a family together. Josh wanted a child of his own as well. That was their plan."

Josh and Angela were together for three years of good times and maybe another year where tensions were rising. In the good times, they both worked hard at their jobs, and the relationship seemed effortless: they were in love. Josh's music was a big part of the picture. Angela would go to all his gigs, and her presence seemed to enhance his performance. He was playing for his internal ear and pleasure; he was playing for the crowd in the room; and he was aware at every moment of her presence in the room. He was creating a sound-track for their most intimate life together.

They functioned as a family of four on weekends, spending time in Jamestown where the boys would play games in the yard or play baseball or football with the kids next door. At least once a month, and in summer more often, the Barbers—including Angela and the boys—would all sit down to dinner together. On every holiday, they were part of the festivities. The four of them were integrated into the extended family of the Barber clan and the Jamestown circle of friends and neighbors. Everyone acted as if Josh and Angela were already married and also treated Nick and Jason as if they were their own two sons. Certainly, Darla and John treated them like grandchildren. There were sleep-overs, birthday parties, presents, and lots and lots of hugs and kisses.

Through all of these good times, however, Josh and Angela still had separate apartments. Josh rented a house in Tiverton on Stafford Pond for about three years, and though Angela and the boys spent a lot of time there, they didn't move in. She still had her own place. When they entertained, it would mostly be at Josh's place. They would have cookouts and bonfires near the water and invite both her family and the Barbers along with friends.

Josh and Angela managed to get away on their own a few times. The boys would stay with Angela's mother. He wanted to take her to Austin to meet his friends there and to be part of the music scene with him. They also had a vacation one year in Florida.

The seeds of tension in the relationship would occasionally become apparent to the family. Josh loved Angela to the point of being possessive at times. She rarely resisted this unspoken yet constant pressure to be always right there for Josh and compliant with his wishes. There were times when the force of his personality was more evident. He could be very demanding, with stern dictates about what he expected from anyone in any kind of a relationship with him. Everyone knew that. Careful observers saw that Josh and Angela were very much in love but that he made these demands upon her too. Early in the relationship with Angela, he insisted that she have a very intimate conversation with Darla. It was nothing that his mother asked for or even welcomed, but Josh felt that Angela had to do this incredibly difficult thing as proof of her honesty, loyalty, and love. Angela was quite upset, but she did what he asked.

Tensions in a family have a way of surfacing over the behavior of children. This family was quite typical. At family dinners in Jamestown, Josh would be the one to discipline the boys over small infractions at the table. He would tell them what they could or could not eat and was more than firm over their protests. Angela would be silent most of the time, and whatever Josh said would stand as the rule. The two adults didn't bicker over these things in front of the boys, but a unilateral, rather than a united, voice is what resulted.

Darla was a little uncomfortable with this one-sided approach. "Sometimes I felt Angela chose loyalty to Josh over her own style of discipline. In this situation, I might have said, 'These are my boys, and I know how to do this!'"

Maggie also noticed the uneven balance of power in the relationship around these issues and other things. "She didn't want to lose him. We knew that she would do anything for Josh because that was the only way that he would truly believe that she cared for and respected him."

Josh was not happy with either his mother or his sister when they stood up for Angela or when they coached a tearful Angela on how to behave. The two women would say, "Angela, you have to stand up for yourself! People treat you the way you let them treat you." Darla would tell Josh that her goal was that they should both be happy. Despite these incidents, they *were* happy; they both assumed that this love affair was "The One." They were fully engaged in each other's lives on a daily basis with great joy and satisfaction and a small measure of tension over seemingly minor issues. They were a good match physically, both of them attractive and socially magnetic, though in different ways. Their career paths, however, were not at all matched.

Josh didn't love his job, but he was a well-respected technician with good upward mobility because of his skills and experience. He earned a good salary and could live comfortably on his own. Angela had two waitressing jobs, and she earned just enough to support herself and the boys. They lived in an apartment complex that didn't seem entirely safe to Josh. Everyone was encouraging her to choose a career and go back to school. Nursing seemed a good choice with assurances of jobs at every level, from the most basic nursing assistant through LPN and RN, and then bachelor's degree qualifications, and so on. It was a ladder with low rungs to get started and then lots of available education to move up the ladder along with flexible hours if she needed them. And nursing salaries were going up with shortages everywhere.

During these same years, when the relationship was on solid ground and the after-hours music career was going strong, Josh's progress at work was steady, but he was still not inspired by his day job. However, the money was good, and he liked the lifestyle where he could take a trip, buy concert tickets or equipment, and party with friends without worrying about breaking his budget. Everything was going smoothly, but in retrospect the possessiveness and demands that were beginning to color his and Angela's relationship were becoming more obvious in other relationships as well.

His friend Chad describes what this period felt like to someone close to Josh during their mid to late twenties. "Around this time I remember Josh becoming a little different. He would get really angry with me for not getting back to him in a timely fashion . . . It was very difficult to reason with him . . . I think it all started from him thinking I would blow him off. And he would never believe me when I tried to convince him otherwise." In Chad's view, there was no cause for Josh to be angry; these were the small issues of any friendship, quickly forgiven and forgotten, but clearly, it felt different to Josh.

Chad and Josh had bought exercise equipment together and often worked out at the end of the day. Now that Chad was out of college and working, he would sometimes have to work late, and this irritated Josh to the point where the young men argued over what it meant to be a friend. Josh felt that Chad wasn't putting enough effort into the relationship. For about a year, the former friends were truly estranged from one another. Chad felt that Josh was even expressing anger at mutual friends for still being friendly with him.

In his journal at around this same time, Josh was having some serious discussions with himself.

> *If everyone knows what's best, why aren't they themselves happy*
> *I haven't met anyone truly happy*
> *I don't know what that takes. I remember these nonspecific times when I was younger and I would have this sudden feeling of complete happiness. Not contentment . . . HAPPINESS and wouldn't be able to keep a smile from my face. Now my forehead aches from a constant scowl. Not purposely, it's just always there. I don't remember the last time I had that feeling.*
>
> *. . .*
>
> *My silence is*
> *The polar opposite of what's*
> *Going on in my head.*
> *So many thoughts.*

Josh was aware of the "constant scowl" that was on his face, instead of the smile he remembers from times of "HAPPINESS," and he also seemed aware that others perceived him as silent even though his head was filled with thoughts.

Life Takes Some Turns

2008 was a big year for J.B. and The Stack. In spring of that year, Chris Conti wrote a short piece under the heading, "Still Smokin," about Josh taking another prize. "Arguably the most competitive category (and chock-full of seasoned veterans), this year's Blues/R&B winner Josh Barber took modesty to the next level when asked if he expected to have a fighting chance against veterans like Paul Geremia and perennial contenders Roomful of Blues. 'No, not at all—everyone is great and probably deserve the award more than me,' Barber stated." Conti goes on to call the group an "apparent underdog" and also notes that they delivered "a consistently scorching live set."

It was also a big year for Josh in several other ways. In March of 2008, he became a government employee at the same facility where his father worked. Those who recruited Josh away from MRC saw great potential in him, and they encouraged him to engage in opportunities to develop his career. Traveling with the USN Torpedo Certification Examining Board team to conduct inspections was one such opportunity. Josh participated in an inspection in Virginia as an "Under Instruction" (UI) team member. Feedback from the certification team's senior member, the USN Torpedo Warrant Holder, and from management personnel working at that location indicated that Josh did a great job and fit in very well. If things continued to go well, he would be invited to perform another "UI" and become a permanent member of the team.

Josh bought a house in Bristol in 2008, and this was another kind of turning point. Young people rent apartments or sometimes rent whole houses, but stable adults with good jobs can support a mortgage and they buy a house. They make the house into a home. It is a commitment to a region and a kind of settling down. Josh did all this, but he didn't go the one step further: he didn't invite Angela and the boys to live with him. He didn't ask her to marry him. This wasn't simply an oversight on his part. It was a decision, whether conscious or unconscious, but still a decision. If they discussed and debated it and made a joint decision, and even if they didn't, the fact of Josh buying a house and moving in on his own was a factor in the relationship. John felt that it was a significant factor that made the struggles between Josh and Angela more extreme and brought them more out in the open.

There is enough momentum in a declining relationship to carry a family through months and months of emotional sniping and indecision until some definitive event blows the remaining shell to bits. Neither Josh nor Angela could imagine breaking up. They both thought that the strong threads in the fabric of their joint life could heal the threads that were weak and even those that had already snapped. If asked, they would each say that they loved one another. The bond between Josh and the two boys was stronger than ever. This was a compelling reason to stay together.

Right around the same time that Josh bought the house in Bristol, Angela made the leap into her own future: she started a nursing program at a local community college. This step didn't look as big as a house, but it was. In fact, it might have been bigger; it opened a door, several windows, and a whole new horizon for Angela. She made a few friends of a different sort than she had connected with in waitressing jobs, and as she began to pass exams and compare her skills and ability with other students, she began to grow in both confidence and self-esteem. She felt the future beginning to open in front of her in a new way. She could see that someday she would not need to be dependent upon anyone. The whole world looks different when you know that you can be self-sufficient financially.

By the summer of 2009, Josh and Angela were both putting in lots of hours at their jobs and then added hours for their other pursuits— music and nursing school—to the point where their relationship was running on autopilot. There were lots of phone calls and text messages of whereabouts and schedules, but fewer and fewer soul mate conversations about life and goals and mutual appreciation. One or the other of them might suddenly show up unwilling to compromise on a given day on a given topic. There was more than tension in the air; they were both downright contentious. Sooner or later, they both sensed, there would be a blow-up. Neither of them knew what the outcome would be.

It started small. Angela knew that there was a No Doubt concert coming up in August. She thought it would be fun to go. This was something that Josh typically loved and that they had done together a number of times before. Because they were not communicating well, neither of them made a genuine effort to discuss the concert and their possible plans as a couple. Angela bought tickets and invited a couple of her new girlfriends to go with her. When Josh found out that she was planning to go without him, he was very upset and angry. He didn't want her to go. "No! No way! You are not going to that concert without me!"

"Well, then come with me." She meant it. Josh was great fun at concerts, and she really wanted him to go.

"No! I'm not going and neither are you!" It was one time too many. Angela had changed enough that this challenge brought out the new woman in her. Her backbone stiffened and she shouted right back. "Yes, I am! I'm going, with or without you. I'll go with my girlfriends."

"If you go, that's the end of us! If you can't do this for me, then we're through!" The threat came out of his mouth so easily. He barely heard himself say it, and he certainly didn't listen for Angela's reply. She fully registered the intimidating warning and took him at his word. It felt so good to shout back at him and then walk away.

Angela went to the concert with her friends, and she and Josh didn't see one another for a couple of weeks afterwards. Nothing was the same after that incident. Josh would send a text or call Angela from time to time and make a plan to get together with the two boys. Both Josh and Angela assumed that the other was dating again. For all practical purposes, they had broken up. On the other hand, Josh seemed to hold on to certain assumptions for the future. He installed bunk beds in his house for the boys, and he bought Xbox games and a foosball table. These actions seemed to point to some thoughts of a future that included Angela and her sons.

Even though Josh had dates with several other women during this period, he still scheduled *guys nights* with the two boys. Their relationship seemed simple; they were tight. One tiny corner of his mind held an image of an intact family living happily in his house in Bristol. Through an extraordinary effort, he kept this vision separate from the more accurate picture of a seriously fractured relationship that was not likely to heal.

The time between August and December 2009 seemed, in some ways, like the formal separation of a married couple. Josh and Angela were learning to live apart. As the holiday season approached, it might have been the first cold snap in late November that pinched Josh to startled awareness that the relationship might be over for good. He invited Angela and the boys to spend Christmas with the Barber family as they had done for the past four or five years, in hopes that the holiday warmth would revive the joyful foursome they had once been.

Children are more than willing to ignore adults' gloomy moods, especially when surrounded by distractions of twinkling lights, candles and tinsel, gifts, and sweets. The veneer of Christmas couldn't hoodwink the adults, however. There was friction in the air, along with a certain dark aura of contained despair. Josh coped by acting like everything was the same this year as in the past, but Darla and John were acutely aware that *nothing* was right between Josh and Angela. All of the adults, including Maggie and the collected grandparents, recognized that it was over. Angela had changed; she seemed stronger and more independent, clearly self-directed toward her career. She was moving on without Josh. There would be no turning back the clock. One week later, she informed Josh that there was a new man in her life.

Josh could no longer push off the impact of the loss. He let it all in and was visibly devastated. The stark picture of a future without Angela and her sons had finally penetrated all the way down to his innermost being. Darla and John witnessed his first moves into a serious depression, but at the time, no one could have predicted the depth and the swiftness of the downward spiral. A few days after Christmas, he called Angela and told her he was going to take pills to end his life. This might have been the very first time he articulated this threat.

Josh was beginning to ask himself, *"How can I live without them?"* He must have been verbalizing this sentiment again in text messages to a friend on New Year's Eve. The friend made an anonymous call to the Bristol police, who showed up at his door minutes later. They searched the house for items that would indicate an actionable intent for self-harm. Finding no obvious preparations, they had no concrete reason to detain him, and so they left. Josh went to bed and slept through the final moments of what had been a traumatic year for him. It was January 1, 2010, when he awoke, but nothing was much changed from the night before.

CHAPTER VI

A New Year

Depression is the flaw in love. To be creatures
who love, we must be creatures who can despair at
what we lose, and depression is the mechanism of that despair.
Andrew Solomon

J OSH NEVER REALLY RECOVERED HIS composure and optimism after all the hustle and bustle around the holidays, along with the clear messages from Angela that she was moving on. He seemed to get more anxious by the day, sometimes at the dark and morose end of the spectrum, and less frequently at the belligerent, red-rage extremity. He would get caught in a particular thought loop, whether it was having Maggie call Angela to plead his case or some new strategy to show her that their life together was worth salvaging. Whatever specific goal he began with would gradually escalate in emotional significance until he was ready to burst with frustration if he couldn't get it done.

One of the things that is known about depression—perhaps not known widely enough—is that it is harder to detect in men. Women are more likely to be diagnosed with depression because they often have more of the classic symptoms and because the symptoms in men may not be recognized as depression. For example, while persistent and disabling feelings of sadness might be an obvious clue, a family might not recognize that irritability and being quick to anger might also be symptoms. A newsletter article issued by Butler Hospital in Providence, Rhode Island, "The Secret Syndrome: Men and Depression," states that "many doctors also believe that depression is at the root of conditions and behaviors, like substance abuse . . . and reckless or risky behavior, such as driving too fast."

Of course, for most families, isolated observations of irritability over months can seem incidental or even specific to a variety of causes and not as a *pattern* of behavior. Even when it does become clear that there is a pattern, it might be this family's first time experiencing such a pattern, and so it might not occur to them that these would be symptoms of a disorder that could have devastating consequences. Dr. James Sullivan, associate medical director of inpatient services at Butler Hospital, is quoted as saying, "men may try to wait out the depression, hoping it will go away on its own. But, untreated depression, much like an untreated infection, becomes worse. Studies have shown that the longer an episode of depression lasts, the worse the symptoms become." Dr. Sullivan is quick to follow this with a reminder that it is *never* too late to seek help toward a recovery.

Josh continued to try to be in touch with Angela in January until, finally, she blocked him from Facebook and any other means of communicating with her online. Darla took this as an opportunity to encourage him to seek some sort of help, perhaps medication for the anxiety and despair that just wouldn't go away. At first he refused, but then it occurred to him that if he did take medication and saw a therapist, perhaps Angela would agree to talk to him and then they could work it out. He reasoned that she would see that he was willing to change and that the most important thing in the world to him was getting back together as a family.

In January, it also became clear that Darla's mother was dying, and she and John decided to spend some time in Maine so they could be with her as much as possible. Josh and Maggie were going about daily routines in Rhode Island. Josh was living alone in Bristol and still working at NUWC, but he was finding it harder to show up five days a week in a productive frame of mind. At about this time, when it seemed things were falling apart, Josh was offered an opportunity to travel to Washington State for an intensive training plan to further his advancement. In the fog of personal crisis, he let this opportunity pass. Maggie was working full time at a new job at Meeting Street Center. She and her boyfriend, Justin Leclerc, were planning to buy a house together. On weekends, Maggie would connect with Josh and try to keep him busy doing something active. Communication lines at this time centered around Maggie; she would text with Josh about plans for the weekend and with her parents about plans with Josh.

On Friday evening, January 15, 2010, as usual, Maggie tried phoning Josh to check in and make plans for the weekend. Josh didn't answer the phone. He almost never answered the phone anymore. She would call him frequently anyway and leave him a message, saying, "Hey, Josh, it's me. I'm just calling to say 'Hi' and see how you are doing. Give me a call back if you feel like it." More and more, Josh didn't want to do anything or talk to anybody.

Maggie thought that Josh would respond via text message, so she texted him. "Justin is going to be busy all day tomorrow, and I have nothing to do! Can you and I do something together?"

"I don't know. I don't care. I don't want to do anything." It was about what she expected, but she continued trying to get him to agree to join her for anything at all. She suggested that she would come to his house, and they could make plans together. Finally he replied, "You can come over if you want; I'm not doing anything."

On Saturday morning, before Maggie left the house for the drive to Bristol, Josh sent her a text message. "I know what we can do today."

"Great! What?" She thought that almost any activity would be positive, but she wasn't expecting what he wrote next: "Buy a ring for Angela."

Maggie wrote back, "I don't think that's a good idea." She tried to persuade her brother to postpone this plan until the two of them were in a happier phase of their relationship. She tried gently to remind him that Angela wouldn't even speak to him on the phone. "This isn't the right time. I think you should wait."

Josh insisted, "I'm going. I'm going without you if you don't want to come."

Maggie knew this would end badly. She couldn't let him go alone, even though she disagreed. She would go along to support him and to be there if, or more likely, when it all crumbled.

The two of them went together to Providence Place Mall. Josh was leading a very purposeful expedition, but he was shaking as if acutely nervous. Maggie followed him from store to store as he looked at rings. It was a surreal experience for her. She felt that this person marching in front of her on a futile search was *not* her brother. Some other consciousness had taken over his body and his voice, and she felt sick with worry about how it was going to play out. They left the mall as soon as he picked out and purchased a ring, and Maggie's apprehension was soon verified.

While driving home from the mall, Josh called Angela and asked if he could see her one more time. From the passenger seat, Maggie was witness to a conversation that was hysterical on both sides. Josh was begging Angela to see him, all the while crying increasingly out of control. Angela was yelling at him from the other end of the connection, "You know I don't want to talk to you! I told you I don't want to talk to you! I don't want to see you; leave me alone!"

Josh pleaded, "Please, just let me see you one more time." He wanted to see her face to face.

Angela insisted, "Whatever you have to say to me, tell me over the phone." She had probably figured out what he wanted to ask her. She said to him "Whatever it is, my answer is going to be 'No!'" Maggie could hear her shouting, "Are you kidding me? I can't believe you're going to do this!"

The desperate pleading continued. Josh couldn't stop sobbing and he continued to repeat, "Please, please! Just let me talk to you!" One of the reasons this sequence felt so devastating is that it was a complete reversal of their roles from better days in the relationship, when

Angela might have been the pleading partner and Josh would have been granting or withholding access or permission. Angela sounded distressed in her new role, Josh was deeply shocked by the turnaround, and Maggie felt a sense of rising panic as they approached the house.

She had been in touch with her parents in Maine, letting them know what was going on. At one point during the day, she wrote to her father, "Dad, I know you are four and a half hours away, but we're going to be in trouble here! I know it's going to end badly, and I'm dealing with this alone, and I don't know what to do."

John was already driving south by the time Josh and Maggie got back to the house in Bristol. Josh got out of the car and went to the lower level living room, where he continued crying and pleading with Angela. Maggie paced upstairs, listening through every pore and muscle of her body to sense where Josh was, if he was still on the phone, and what his emotional condition might be.

When Josh finally got off the call with Angela, there was a silent pause throughout the house. A few moments later, Josh came upstairs to the kitchen, still sobbing quietly. Maggie thought he was depleted from the tension of the shopping trip all morning and then the crazed exchange with Angela over the phone, but that wasn't the case. Josh entered the room and with an angry roar, he put his fist right through the wall. He pulled his hand out from the shattered drywall and went on a rampage, flipping over the table and trying to rip cabinet doors off hinges.

Maggie was stunned and a little fearful. She had never seen this person before. This wasn't her brother. Still, she believed deep in her heart that Josh would never hurt her, and so she followed him as he paced around the house and out to the yard. All the while, he was shouting at her to leave, but she stayed firm. "I'm not leaving. I'm staying here with you. It's going to be OK."

John arrived while Josh was still agitated. He and Maggie calmed Josh enough to get him to sit down, but clearly the battle was still going on inside. He rocked back and forth with his head in his hands, repeating through his sobs, "I can't believe she's gone. I can't believe she doesn't love me anymore. I don't know what I'm going to do without them. They're all I want! She's all I have!'"

His father tried to reach through the pain and pull his son back from the emotional storm. "Josh! Snap out of it! I want you to cut this bullshit and pull yourself together!"

John and Maggie continued to talk and reason with him for another hour, but when they realized that he was not improving, they made the very tough decision to take him to a hospital.

Maggie emphasized the physical injury to her brother; they needed to go and get x-rays of the hand which was swollen and red by this time. She also offered that they would ask for some medication to ease his anxiety. In her mind, the emotional storm was the main reason they were seeking emergency care. "Listen, Josh, they can give you something at the hospital to help you chill out and come down from this."

John was very direct. "Put your shoes on. We're going to the hospital!"

Maggie typed the word *hospital* into her GPS, and they drove directly to the nearest emergency facility at Saint Anne's Hospital in Fall River, Massachusetts. Josh was tense and rigid while waiting, but he had calmed himself and was no longer crying. He was even able to tell the doctor that he had broken up with his girlfriend, and because he was so pissed off, he put his hand through the wall. No bones were broken, and as a result of Maggie's explanation to the nurse off to the side, he was given a prescription for Xanax for his anxiety. After he was treated and released, the three of them went back to Bristol in the early hours of the morning.

This was the first time for so many of the feelings that would overwhelm the Barber family in the coming months: the feeling that a situation was completely out of control; that this was not the Josh they knew; and the feeling that if they could all get through this one crisis, things would get better. The prescription Josh received on this occasion was the first of many. From this moment on, his sister and parents would not know how much of his emotional roller coaster and erratic behavior was brought on by his struggles to cope with life's disappointments and how much by unfortunate effects of various medications and his compliance or not with recommended doses and schedules.

Josh's extreme agitation and anger would again lead to acting out and even more disturbing scuffles. As much as possible in each case, a family member would intervene to limit the harm done. The destructive cycle would be followed by positive actions to repair damages. In this case, Josh's composure and patience in patching the wall he had broken led his family to believe that he was recovering from an isolated outburst. They felt optimistic that the danger was past and better times were ahead.

An e-mail exchange between John and Josh on January 19, 2010, with the subject heading "Passion" provides a clear view of how a father tries to reason with his desperately unhappy and isolated son. "Josh . . . e-mail is not a substitute for talking to a real person, but you leave me no alternative. Ever since hockey, you have been obsessive about the things you do. That's also when you stopped being a full time happy person (when you lost hockey). It's also when you transitioned from a boy to a man, which had a bit to do with it."

John urges his son to recognize the difference between being *passionate* about life, a positive quality, and being *obsessed*, a potentially destructive way of being. Urging Josh to seek out the pleasure of passion through making music and finding a loving relationship with another woman, John offers both comforting assurances and stern imperatives. "Do something to recover . . . You're young and handsome, you have a house and a good job . . . You're a rock star . . . Suck it up and get on with it." John ends the message with good humor and with a lightly veiled request for his son to communicate with him, and then he signs off with love.

Josh replied ten hours later with just three words, "I appreciate it."

Another Family Crisis

While Darla spent much of the second half of January in Maine, John and Maggie were staying with Josh. During the days that she was gone, Josh called his mother frequently, sometimes crying so hard she couldn't understand what he was saying. She could make out the theme of every call, however, and it was always the same—he didn't want to go on living if he couldn't repair his relationship with Angela. Darla could hear John or Maggie in the background of some calls, speaking softly and trying to comfort Josh. He was inconsolable over the loss of the relationship, and Darla tried her best to summon the energy and the right words to ease his pain. She would turn from these calls to bring her best self to lift her mother's spirits, meanwhile wondering if she could sustain this double drain on her own inner strength. The mother and the daughter in her were both being summoned to extreme crisis, and she had to keep a firm hand on her emotions, or she would break down and not be able to help her mother achieve a good death or Josh achieve a good life.

Darla returned to Jamestown for a few days when her mother seemed stable, only to get a call that she had taken a turn and might live just another day or two. John and Darla together drove up to Maine immediately, and all the siblings were with their mother when she died on January 31, 2010.

Strong traditions and rituals take over a family's actions immediately after a death, especially of a matriarch like Doris Snow. Actual grieving is often postponed by the rituals themselves, and some never do set aside time to mourn after the funeral.

Maggie and Josh, if he was able, were planning to drive to Maine for the funeral. Josh was not doing so well at this time, but he wanted to drive his own car up to Maine. Maggie acquiesced and rode along as a passenger, although she felt that she was managing everything about the trip and that he was entirely in her care. "Perhaps the focus required to drive four and a half hours will be good for Josh," she reasoned. Josh talked about Angela for the entire ride up to Maine.

He was absorbed in reflecting on how their relationship had been so solid for so long, and he hadn't realized what a gamble he was taking when he put that on the line. He loved her and had always loved her. He would love her forever no matter what happened because they were meant to be together. Maggie responded with brief comments and observations, simply agreeing in hopes that he would feel validated and then move on to another topic, or trying to draw his attention, even momentarily away from the past.

Darla was very happy to see Josh at the family gatherings before and after the funeral. He was with all of his cousins, and this seemed to lift him out of the doldrums that had followed them up from Rhode Island. Josh loved family, and he seemed more than willing to pick up his guitar to play and sing for them. Although he was talking and smiling and interacting with everyone, underneath it all, his deep sadness was still evident.

Josh and his cousin Stevie connected with a big hug and picked up their banter as if they had been together every day for months. Stevie was a phenomenal source of strength for Josh. He was caring and loving and brutally honest. He also made Josh laugh as no one else in the world could. When Darla and John saw Josh with Stevie and the others, they allowed themselves to hope that he was turning a corner.

Maggie was seeing a different view of the situation. She had been with Josh in the car for over four hours on the way up. She knew he was extremely anxious, and she noticed that his hands and legs were shaking. There was a quality of unrest about the way he couldn't sit still, couldn't pause and just be. He was not in good shape. Maggie didn't know if Josh's state of agitation was brought on by recent events or, possibly, by the prescription medication he was taking. Late in the day, after the funeral, when all the family was together, Josh left the room. "Where did Josh go? Have you seen Josh?" Maggie was worried.

He had decided that he couldn't stay the night as planned, and he was about to leave without a word to anyone. All the emotion of the gathering had become too much for him, and he couldn't stay any longer. Maggie tried to reason with him. "Why don't we stay the night? We could get up and leave early in the morning."

"No. I want to go. I'm going! If you want to stay, you can come home with Mom and Dad."

Maggie could see that he was not going to be persuaded by any arguments. He was leaving immediately, and she decided to go along with him. They drove back to Bristol that night, and Maggie stayed overnight at Josh's house. She was exhausted, not only from the long, long day and the hours in the car, but also from the press of sorrow at her grandmother's passing and, most of all, from being on the receiving end of the incredible waves of anxiety that radiated outward from Josh.

January and February were hard months for all four Barbers. Darla had turned from her mother's deathbed to help plan the funeral, and then her attention was focused, once again, almost exclusively on Josh. She was heavy with grief but never gave herself the luxury of grieving. Meanwhile, Josh was struggling with anxiety that at times seemed to be a speeding eighteen-wheeler aimed right at him. When he wasn't completely absorbed with working on his car, or finding the exact right lyrics and chords for a song, he would start a long, slow spiral down to dark places. He couldn't see his way out to any future at all, and he would often call one of his parents or his sister, sobbing in near-hysteria.

A positive activity that occupied a good bit of Josh's attention in these months was looking for a dog. He had convinced himself that, given recent events, he would never have a family or children, so he might as well seek the closest thing to it. He did some research online and thought that he might want an English bulldog. As with many things in this period, his family was involved in the process. Darla would go with Josh to visit various pet stores to look at puppies. He was also finding out about dog breeders where he could purchase a puppy directly. Everyone was keeping an eye out for just the right dog for Josh. One day Darla saw what she thought was an English bulldog with its owner in Wickford. She took the time to engage the man in conversation and found out it was, indeed, the breed that Josh was thinking of. Her overall impression was not good. "Josh, I saw an English bulldog today, and you don't want that dog! It's big and very slobbery." And, they had learned, very expensive. The search went on.

One day, Josh and Darla were in yet another pet store, and they found they couldn't take their eyes off a tiny black puppy that yipped a greeting to them as if they were old friends or kindred spirits. Darla almost bought him on the spot, and she told Josh if he didn't get this dog, she was going to. This little ball of energy was a pug, and he was just as expensive as the bulldog, despite his minuscule size and his weight in mere ounces.

Unlike his usual impulsive self, Josh now became very deliberate about this decision. He asked lots of questions about the breed and about this particular puppy. Even though they both felt their heart strings tugged, they left the store without buying the dog. A few days later, when Josh's cousin Stevie was visiting him, Darla received a photo of the little dog that had just joined the family. She felt relieved that Josh had filled a void in his life and would have a warm body to cuddle with, to take care of, and to fill his house with joyful noise. It was a hopeful moment and she let herself believe that it signaled a transition toward new interests and away from dwelling on the past.

Josh engaged the whole family and many of his friends in the process of naming the puppy. The little ball of fur inspired plenty of possible names, but it finally came down to two that were inspired by his music: *Austin* for Austin, Texas, or *Doyle* after Josh's idol, Doyle Bramhall II. The dog had such an energetic nature that Josh settled on naming him after the city where he had felt totally alive among like-minded and like-talented folks. Now that he had a constant companion, Josh set about training him with all the love he had been saving up for children. Austin absorbed most of Josh's attention and affection with keen intelligence, and he returned it all in good measure.

At first, Austin could scarcely climb over the half step from the deck into the kitchen, but Josh taught him how to hit the screen with his paw and then slide it open to come in. Austin learned all about treats and how to get them by giving his paw or rolling over. At night, Josh lifted him up to sleep at the foot of his bed. They were inseparable; Josh referred to Austin as his wingman.

One Saturday during this period, Maggie was spending the day with Josh, trying to keep him busy and distracted by doing errands. Any little thing she needed to pick up or drop off could provide a reason for them to drive around to this or that store, just to get out of the house for a change of scenery and perhaps a change of mood.

For most of the morning, their conversation centered on whether Josh and Angela would be able to renew their relationship. Maggie inserted some gentle reminders that it would be good for Josh to think realistically about the possibility that maybe they wouldn't get back together. He would move on with his life. Maggie enjoyed having such a frank discussion with her brother; it felt like real progress; it felt like the real Josh. He even had the ability to divert himself from his own pain to think about his sister. "I don't want to bother you with all my stuff, Maggie. I'm going to be fine."

She was moved by his comment but wanted him to understand the depth of her commitment. "I'm so thankful to be your friend again and to be spending time with you. I will listen to you all day. I'm your sister. This is what I'm here for. Thank God we have each other again!"

After they had gone to the drug store, department store, and video game store, Maggie began suggesting some ideas for the rest of the day, but Josh had something else on his mind. He wanted Maggie to call Angela and persuade her to come to his house with the boys. Angela wasn't answering his calls anymore, but he thought she might answer a call from Maggie. He begged, "I really just want to see the boys. Honestly, I don't even care whether she comes or not."

Maggie was disappointed at this twist to the day's agenda. "Josh, where is that going to get us? What if she says she's not coming over?"

He kept saying, "I just want to see the boys. It will make me feel better. They always make me happy. I miss them so much. I don't need to see Angela; you do something with Angela." Shifting the focus away from Angela was very persuasive. Maggie felt that it might be a healthy thing for him to spend time with the boys and lift his spirits a bit.

Maggie finally called and explained the whole situation. In addition, she was very blunt with her brother's former girlfriend, telling her, "If you know in your heart that the two of you have no future, then please don't come! Don't bring the boys, and don't drag this out. We are trying to help Josh figure out how to move on. If there is hope for the relationship, we'll support him in trying, in a healthy manner, to piece things back together."

Angela decided to accept the invitation.

While the women cooked dinner, Josh played outside with the boys. It was cold out, but the three of them were running around, throwing the football and tumbling on the ground. The boys were shouting and calling his name, and Josh was smiling. Looking out the sliding doors from the kitchen to the yard, Maggie felt a sense of relief that Josh was having such carefree fun. The afternoon felt like an oasis from all the recent turmoil, and she allowed herself to feel optimistic.

When Josh and the boys came in, they all sat down and had dinner together and then went downstairs and watched TV for a short while. There didn't seem to be much tension between Josh and Angela; they were cordial to one another but not warmly affectionate in the slightest. They were pleasant like acquaintances or long-time battling lovers on a truce. About an hour after dinner, Angela and the boys left. It had been an agreeable family evening, and both Maggie and Josh felt their spirits lifted by the visit. Josh gained a small measure of comfort from doing ordinary things together just like a normal family, and this made the next few days a little easier. About a week later, this illusion was shattered when Angela let him know that she was going on a date with someone else.

Inner Pain, Outer Turmoil

In February, 2010, Josh wrote the following entry in his journal.

I guess it's time for another entry of pain and sadness. Another Chapter? All others meant so much to me, especially at the time. But now, this one means more than any. Through this crippling separation, perhaps I've started to find help? What started as a relationship plagued with obstacles and pain. Hurdles I never thought I could climb over. Yet years passed and the bond grew stronger than any that I've ever felt. So much so that I thought we would be together forever no matter what. We both found ourselves (I think?) Through my lack of support and show of appreciation, you stood up. You grew a spine, and more importantly your dignity. And I'm so proud of you. You have always been so full of love for everyone else around you—yet had none for yourself. I guess that goes for both of us.

As always, I wish things were different. So many great memories, and I wasted so many chances to make things better. And I accept responsibility for that. But as we all know now, and as this book serves as evidence of a seriously troubled soul, perhaps I truly was unable [to grow] without losing you. So with the end you and I have a new beginning. One where we both have learned more about ourselves than we ever knew before.

Unfortunately, it took the greatest pain and loss I've ever felt. You were my soul mate. We thought the same. We finished each other's sentences. You were my wife in my eyes. And the two boys who'd been robbed of a real father became my sons. Therefore we were a family. A family full of turmoil. Much of which I created. But the love was ALWAYS there. I always loved you more than anything in the world.

I became dependent on you for sanity. You were my drug, as others have been before. But the loss of those other drugs was never great enough to admit I needed help. Never enough to give in to my pride and admit something wasn't quite right.

But you were. Although I needed to do it for me, I was motivated by you. I'd have done anything to get you back.

And I did. Everything I could. And the more I fell apart, the meaner you got. I was too late. During the 6 months that passed after the breakup, I was unaware of your reality. You were at wits end, and forced into getting through what I had faced you with. And with each passing day got closer to closure . . . while I was getting closer and closer to realizing what I had done.

Yet I was too stupid to realize this time may be different than all the others. This time you were going to stand up. I always thought we'd be together no matter what. And took it for granted as I did so many other things with having you in my life.

So here I am. Happier having received help. Happier having gained a new love and appreciation for my family's support. But broken inside over the loss of my family of 3.

I think we both changed each other's lives for the better in the end. I just wish it could've ended with us together after realizing all that we have.

But sometimes it's too late. And sometimes people fall out of love. And the most surreal part for me was seeing you look into my eyes and realizing your love was gone.

The most loving person I knew, for the first time had dried up. Your love was gone. Cold.

I don't know what the future holds. I just hope you and the boys are happy. I love the three of you so much, all I care about is that you're happy, healthy, and taken care of—even if that's without me . . .

Darla and John moved in with Josh in Bristol in early March after several months of escalating crisis. John would go to work almost every day in Newport, but Josh wasn't capable of sustaining the focus needed to work. His human resources supervisor at NUWC was very compassionate and facilitated all the available leave allowances. Many of John's colleagues donated multiple days of their own leave to Josh's account so he would receive a paycheck for as long as possible.

John took heart from the birthday card that Josh gave him with a photo of a child's hand gripping a strong adult hand. "Dad," he wrote above the printed greeting card message of "I may not need you to hold my hand anymore—but I'll always need you to hold me in your heart." Below "Happy Birthday," Josh added, "There are no words to express my appreciation for the help and support you have given me through all this lately. All three of you came to my rescue, and I'd have been gone by now if you hadn't. I love you. JOSH"

Darla would spend lots of days at home with Josh, trying to interest him in little outings, anything to lift his spirits and distract him from his constant fiddling with the iPhone and constant access to Facebook on his computer.

One night in early March, the Barbers planned to have a family dinner together. It was a warmish day, and it felt like winter might be over. Darla and Josh had spent a pleasant afternoon at several antique stores and consignment shops. He knew she loved browsing around, and he was feeling energetic enough to initiate an outing that he knew would please her. The plan was that Maggie would meet them at The Backyard Grill, right across the street from Josh's house, after work, and they would have dinner when John arrived after his day.

The context of this evening for Josh included saying, earlier that day, a somewhat final goodbye to the two little boys he had once thought would be his family forever. In between shopping with Darla and meeting for dinner, he had taken several lorazepam to dampen his anxiety.

Maggie met Josh and Darla after work, and the three of them sat at the bar to have a drink and wait for John. Over the course of about an hour, Josh sat with the two women, communicating fully, but at the same time, completely immersed in some activity on his iPhone. They couldn't see what he was doing, whether he was texting someone or whether he was on Facebook, but his attention was more on the iPhone than on them or anything else around him. This was very typical for Josh around this time and very troubling for his mother and sister.

Darla noticed that Josh's combination of scotch and medication that afternoon was not going well. "We had a drink and the plan was to have dinner, but Josh decided he didn't want to eat, although he did want more to drink. He got somewhat agitated when Maggie and I didn't want to stay at the bar any longer. The afternoon and night went downhill from there. I assume he had taken some medication, in addition to the drinks of Crown Royal. His behavior became more and more agitated."

Josh's primary care physician had prescribed Adderall, thinking perhaps that he had a form of ADHD or that it would help with the depression. Darla and John felt that Josh really didn't need it. Maggie agreed. He also had a prescription for lorazepam. "I think he took Adderall to give himself a little boost because he was feeling so crappy all the time. The doctors prescribed it, and he took it, and he was much more agitated when he did."

Over the course of the next thirty minutes or so—whether it was due to Adderall, lorazepam, the couple of drinks that he had, what he was looking at on his phone, or the combination—Josh got more and more agitated. Finally, he got up and abruptly left the bar, crossing the street and entering his house. Darla and Maggie became increasingly anxious, and the same thought went through their minds: *"Is this the night when things get completely out of control?"*

By the time they paid the bill and crossed the street, Josh was sitting in the back yard, talking on the phone. Just then, John pulled into the driveway in his truck and parked behind Josh's car. Darla had phoned him with an update on the situation, and he anticipated that Josh might try to drive off. Josh was in no condition to drive. Many of their encounters with Josh had had a similar sequence: one or two of the family at the house with a very anxious and agitated Josh waiting for the other(s) to arrive. Then they would huddle in extreme apprehension and wonder what to do next. The common factor of so many of these situations was that Josh pushed them away. If they wouldn't leave, he would flee from them.

One time, on a similar night, John blocked Josh's car with his truck. Josh knew where his father hid the spare key, and he quickly retrieved it and drove off in the truck. This time, he took off on foot after rejecting John's several attempts to divert him from his distress or even to have a conversation.

The three were frantic, worrying that he would immediately seek to harm himself or that in his state of extremity, he would provoke some fatal confrontation. They felt so alone with the thought of these imminent dangers. Maggie had called the police just a few days before and asked them what the options were for help in such situations. The answer sounded so easy. "He can either come to the hospital voluntarily with you, or you can call the police and he'll be transported involuntarily to the hospital."

Now her brother was sprinting away from them through neighborhood streets under the influence of a cocktail of drugs, alcohol, and social media, and they felt desperate for help and yet completely distressed at the thought of calling the police.

Darla stayed at the house in case Josh should return, and John and Maggie went out in the truck searching for him. They drove all around his neighborhood in a panic. Not knowing the area, John followed a strange intuition of where to look. They drove down a dead-end road in the neighborhood, down near the water, and there he was. It was shocking to see him standing there in the headlights with the water right behind him.

Maggie and John got out of the truck and did all they could to convince Josh to get in the truck and to come back home with them. He was completely irrational, shouting incoherently one second and sobbing the next. Maggie was nearly as distraught, finding it hard to grasp that this was happening in her family, in her life. Her legs were shaking. They were so desperate and felt they had nobody to help. They didn't know what to do to keep Josh safe.

He wouldn't listen to reason, not to Maggie's pleading nor to John's commands. Finally, John tried to force Josh to get in the truck, and they wrestled briefly. Josh simply would not cooperate. He slipped away and ran off into the woods.

John and Maggie got in the truck and drove back to the house. They both felt traumatized by the intensity of the altercation with Josh. Maggie couldn't stop saying, "What are we going to do? Where is he going? What are we going to do?"

John had just been grappling with his grown son, and he now fought off tears. "I'm finished. I chased him. I struggled with him. He's irrational; there's nothing I can do!"

Darla listened to both of them and seemed ready to take a more active role. "John, you stay here! Come on, Maggie! We're going out there to find Josh!" When Darla is determined, no one argues. Maggie got her car keys, and they set out in her car this time.

After driving up and down the nearby streets, they finally encountered Josh walking along the side of the road with a long piece of jagged metal in his hand. Darla got out of the car and talked to him, while Maggie drove slowly alongside them. Darla could tell that Josh was not himself at all. "We argued. I told him we needed to go back to the house. He kept telling me 'Call the police!' When I asked him why, he said, 'let them come and get me!' He was insisting in his anger, but I wouldn't call them. I knew why he wanted them to come."

Darla was very calm but forceful. She knew that he wanted to provoke a confrontation with the police that would put an end to his suffering. She felt sure that he just wanted it to be over.

It was getting very cold out, and Josh wasn't wearing a coat. Perhaps he just got exhausted. Maybe it was something that Darla said, or maybe he just gave in, but eventually, he got in the car, and Maggie drove back to the house. Josh didn't seem to know what to do or what was going to happen next. Neither did anyone else.

Darla got out of the car and went into the house to tell John what was going on, that they had Josh with them and what he was saying. Josh wouldn't get out of the car, and Maggie wouldn't leave him alone, so the two of them just sat there. "Just call the police! Call the fucking police!" He kept badgering his sister.

"Why? Josh, we love you, and we're here to help you. Why would we call the police? Let's just go inside. We'll stay with you until you feel better." He rejected the idea of taking any medication, but he did respond to her question about why he was insisting that they call the police.

"They will finish what I can't do." His vision, as pieced together later, was that when the police responded to the call, he would threaten them with the piece of metal he had in his hand and they would shoot and kill him. There is even a term for this strategy: "suicide by police."

At last, Josh got out of the car, and they went into the house. He still didn't want to be around his family, so he went down to the basement. Darla kept checking on him, and it wasn't long before he tried to sneak out through the garage. John rushed out and restrained him. Josh was strong, and he was bigger and taller than John, so it was a very risky move to hold him when he was determined to leave. Darla was screaming at Josh as she tried to help John control him. They had reached the breaking point. Maggie was sobbing as she dialed 911.

The sirens and flashing blue and red lights came quickly. Police pulled up in front of the house, separated the family members, and asked each of them questions about what had happened.

Josh was very angry even though he had been saying, "Call the police! Call the police!" He didn't realize what process would be set in motion as soon as they were called. They took Josh to the police station and left the other three sitting at the house, in shock and wondering what was happening to Josh. Who would take care of him now?

Mandatory and Involuntary

The police evaluated the situation as they had observed it and as reported by all four Barbers, and then they transported Josh to Rhode Island Hospital. Maggie, Darla, and John spent much of the night calling the hospital and then the police department over and over, trying to figure out where Josh was. When they first called Rhode Island Hospital, the person on the line wouldn't confirm anything. In fact, Maggie was told that he wasn't there. When she called the police department, they assured her that they had dropped him off there, and when she called the hospital again, they told her that he was *not* there.

Finally someone came to the phone who would give them verification that Josh was indeed there. They were told that there was really nothing they could do overnight, that they wouldn't be allowed to see him where he was, and that the social worker would call them in the morning after he was evaluated.

Josh's mother, father, and sister were left feeling utterly devastated that this was happening in the most wonderful family they could imagine. John and Darla had tried to be unconditionally loving and supportive parents. Maggie knew that no one of them would ever be alone to go through any bad experience in life. She hated the fact that the police had taken her brother, and that he was by himself, and that they couldn't be there with him. In fact, even if they were by his side, they couldn't be having the same experience Josh was having that night. He was alone with the surge of his emotions, and keeping him safe wasn't the same thing as surrounding him with the security of their love.

Darla and John were drained and silent after the physical and emotional struggle with their son. Maggie's mind kept circling around the same thoughts: "How did this happen? How did we get to this point?"

Out of options and at their wits' end, the Barbers had called the police to try to protect Josh from his own self-destructive impulses. The Bristol police performed all the functions of first responders with a swift arrival, on-the-spot investigation, and enough force to impose security and safety on a full-grown man intent on harming himself. Given the circumstances of the evening, reports from Darla, John, and Maggie, and a professional evaluation, the police transported Josh to Rhode Island Hospital for a mandatory, involuntary psychiatric commitment of five days.

Maggie took the phone call. She was sleeping on and off, directly on the floor next to her plugged-in cell phone. She was the one making all the calls, trying to get updates on what was going on. In between making calls and waiting for calls, she dozed lightly for an hour or two at a time. When the phone rang with news of his hospital admission, she felt a sense of relief based on nothing more than her conviction that Josh would now receive the help he needed to escape from the nightmare he had been living for months.

The Barbers had no previous experience with inpatient mental health facilities. They didn't even know anyone who had. Josh's first hospitalization was an unwelcome education for all of them. When they arrived to visit Josh the first day, they were surprised at how many of their expectations from the movies of what a psychiatric ward was like were accurate. The unit was locked. Visitors would get off the elevator and wait at the door where a staff member would ask questions, sign them in, and unlock the door. When his mother, father, and sister arrived at Josh's room, he was sitting on his bed in his underwear and hospital gown. They were disturbed to see their bright young son/brother stripped of the common dignity of his own clothing. There were barefoot patients walking around in their hospital gowns and robes, some of them gazing blankly out of the tiny windows. Despite the environment and his minimal attire, Josh seemed completely back to his normal self, and he told them, decisively, that he wanted to go home. "Let's figure this out so I can get out of here! What do we have to do?"

It was clear to his family that Josh didn't belong with the cohort on this unit. Already he was so much better than the previous night when the combination of alcohol and Adderall may have tipped his distress in such an alarming direction. He was prevented from using any electronic devices on the ward, and thus he had no phone, no text messages, and no Facebook to stimulate his intense emotions. He seemed to be back to his usual self, both funny and compassionate, and focused on the immediate goal of being released.

The circumstances of his admission required that the hospital keep him under observation for five days. There was nothing any of them could do to negotiate a release before then. At the end of the five days, the legal options would be for Josh to sign in voluntarily for additional treatment, for the hospital to discharge him, or, if warranted, for the hospital to seek a court hearing and a further period of involuntary commitment. Josh quickly realized that his fastest route out of the hospital was to cooperate fully with all personnel and treatment so that he could be declared no longer a suicide risk and be released at the end of the five days.

It was a difficult five days. There appeared to be just one inpatient ward at this hospital for a range of psychiatric issues, including severe disability and suicide prevention. All personal belongings were removed, including clothing for the first few days. Josh could not have his guitar or even a pencil to draw or write with. Surveillance was constant. To Maggie, it felt like her brother was being punished for needing help. "It felt to me like they were making a point by keeping his things from him, like they were trying to teach him a lesson."

The protocols are put in place to ensure the safety of patients, but they leave families feeling that their loved one may be in danger from the very harsh measures designed for institutional functioning. The atmosphere, according to John, was not conducive to healing or improvement. "The mental health care system is broken! They just throw you in this box. There can be no progress, unless you happen to have a rare and extraordinary professional on your case."

Darla, John, and Maggie visited Josh every day. After a few days, they were allowed to bring Josh some magazines and drawing materials that were carefully inspected before being given to him. When visiting hours were over, Darla, John, and Maggie would have to leave Josh in a place that was the opposite of all their instincts of how to help him. The only positive that could be taken from this experience was that it might serve as a deterrent, like the threat of imprisonment. They were sick with worry about a possibly violent roommate and the overall effects of the whole environment.

Josh wrote about the experience and made sketches as soon as he was allowed pencil and paper. He expressed the desperation of being "locked up," as he called it, in a short poem. The setting is the top floor of the oldest part of the brick hospital building along Route I-95. It was renovated as a secure indoor/outdoor recreation area for psychiatric patients. The windows had been replaced with chain link fence to allow air to circulate, and the floor was covered with synthetic turf. Patients were allowed to go out there several times each day to play soccer or walk around.

> *Left without the shirt on my back,*
> *I sit timid like a foreigner in a new world,*
> *Through a haze, the night's chaos drifts in and out*
> *All I can focus on is the quickest way out.*
> *Like a rat in a cage, more than ever aware of my age*
> *These freaks aren't me, they got the wrong guy.*
> *An accidental clear spot amongst cloud filled sky,*
> *Let me out before I crack.*
> *Time drags on, while life flies by outside this window*
> *Freedom gains new meaning. I long to just*
> *Touch grass or lay down on it. Every breeze through*
> *Chain linked fence is a gift.*

Josh had regained his composure rather quickly with the shock of mandatory hospitalization and the absence of any Internet or phone service. Once he got his clothes back, it was difficult to tell that he was a patient and not one of the staff or perhaps a community volunteer providing social activities for the patients. He became part of a social group unlike any of his previous relationships. In only one way was it similar: Josh's style of connecting and his feelings of empathy for these people were just as strong as he had always felt for others. On the ward Jane Brown 5 South, his associations included a delusional woman who believed she owned the hospital and that all the visitors were there for her. She wore arts and crafts glitter on her face like make-up. One elderly male patient was so painfully shy that he never looked up, and a burly, heavily-medicated man was reputed to have been a ferocious gang member. Another patient took Josh under his wing to show him the ropes, and Josh bonded with a cognitively disabled eighteen-year old boy. He cared about them all and when his own family visited, he told them the life stories and troubles of all these people.

Josh tried to cooperate with every rule, regulation, and treatment. He went to all of the assigned group therapy sessions and took his medication as ordered—except for the one time when a nurse tried to force him to take additional medication and he yelled at her. He was fully alert and recognized that he had already taken his usual dose. Upon pressing the point, he learned that the doctor had increased his dose without telling him. This might have worked for many on the floor, but Josh was not impaired at this point, and he resented being treated in this way by a psychiatrist who visited him for ten minutes a day. Josh's strategy was to be on his best behavior so as to be released at the earliest possible moment when the mandatory period was over. This required a great deal of restraint because he felt that care givers either did not listen to him or they discounted whatever he said. He was trapped in exchanges where his words were undermined by the very fact of his location in this place. Outside that locked door, his statements might have meaning; inside the door, he might have been speaking nonsense.

The Barbers celebrated Maggie's birthday on March 7th at Rhode Island Hospital with Josh. They sang "Happy Birthday" to her in the common room surrounded by other patients. Maggie's gift from Josh was a pencil sketch of the view from his window of three tall smokestacks.

As Josh's mandatory stay was concluding, a family meeting was scheduled with his attending psychiatrist to discuss whether Josh was ready to go home. Family input was invited, and Josh was given the opportunity to comment, but the final decision would be up to the doctor. The worst possible outcome would be for the doctor to conclude that Josh needed a further period of involuntary hospitalization. John, Darla, and Maggie knew that Josh had been making every effort to be compliant, but they also knew that he was quick to anger and had a vigorous style of speech that some might perceive as belligerent. "I'm ready to get out of this place!" Josh directed his gaze at the doctor. "I'm not getting a single benefit from being treated like a caged animal in here."

The doctor immediately responded. "You're free to walk around wherever you want." His comment sounded defensive and not quite true, since there were locked doors at every entrance and exit of the ward. It crossed Maggie's mind that this was a test. She didn't know if her brother was reading the signals, but she felt strongly that the doctor was not really making a statement but rather a chess move to see how Josh would react. Josh was alert and ready for evasive moves, and he countered with the obvious. "Wherever I want? Sure! The doors are locked."

The question and answer session went around the table a few times, with Darla or John or Maggie commenting on how they would provide support and Josh providing textbook answers about his motivation to get back to his routines and responsibilities. The psychiatrist gave off an attitude of knowing better than they did about everything—about whether they were concealing anything from him or from themselves, about the value of the ward's atmosphere and policies, even about who they were as individuals and as a family.

This was particularly maddening as, despite several phone calls, they had not been able to schedule any interim consultations with him about Josh's progress.

The family meeting reached a crisis at one point, when the doctor challenged the involvement of Josh's parents and sister in his life. He asked, "Why are you three here today?" This question surprised them. Darla, John, and Maggie thought that their closeness as a family was a positive factor in all of their lives. Yet, here was a medical professional questioning their involvement as if it might be a part of the problem. "Who decided that Josh needed to be in the hospital? Did he make that call? No, one of you did that."

All four of them stared at him. Their shock and outrage must have been clear on their faces, but he continued with a final thrust of the knife. "This is not a healthy family situation. In no way are you helping your son. You are *enmeshed!*" He released the term as if spilling a bucket of piranha into the room.

The doctor held all the cards. He could release their son or take his case to a judge. No one wanted the latter to happen, so they deflected the attack and made positive comments about the constant love and support that were typical in their family. In the moment, they were focused on succeeding with their immediate goal. Later, this comment would sting more and more, as they thought about the whole meeting and the arrogance of the doctor's approach.

A second flashpoint occurred when Josh mentioned his interactions with the other patients. He commented that one good outcome of his stay was that he felt he had been able to comfort and encourage other patients. He gave an example of defending one patient when another patient was trying to take advantage of him. Josh also believed that his music and his outgoing nature had brought some life back into their eyes. The doctor listened for a couple of sentences, and then interrupted Josh, saying "They were all doing just fine before you got here."

Both Maggie and Darla were processing this exchange with the benefit of their own training in human services. The patient (Josh) seemed to be able to focus on others with great empathy, even while recovering from his own acute distress. This seemed like a good thing until the doctor pounced on and diminished Josh's efforts with a belittling statement. It almost seemed that he was jealous of Josh's connection with the other patients. In Maggie's eyes, this was an opportunity to reinforce positive self-image in someone who was struggling with depression and self-destructive impulses. She was horrified at both the words and the tone directed at her brother by this physician who held so much power over his life at this particular moment.

The four Barbers left the contentious meeting feeling extremely offended by the whole condescending atmosphere created by the very professional who was responsible for ensuring a safe and healing environment. They felt he had been manipulative, dismissive, and cruel. It should not have been a surprise, however, that he would conduct such an unsatisfying family meeting: his brief encounters with Josh all week had also been abrupt and confrontational. This session was the capstone of their first experience with inpatient mental health care, and it shaped their perspective that some potentially therapeutic occasions can, instead, turn out to be quite the opposite.

Looking back upon the experience, Maggie reflected that Josh was not an easy patient to categorize. Once he got beyond the acute phase of his extreme anxiety, his intelligence and vibrant personality would reappear. He was not ill in the way a person with diabetes or Lou Gehrig's disease is ill. There would be no predictable progression of his symptoms, and there would be no guaranteed therapeutic protocol. Most of the time, he was completely sane by any definition of that term. With the flip of a switch, it seemed, he would be incapacitated and nearly deranged with anxiety, panic, and hopelessness. The switch was almost any reminder of his failed relationship.

Josh had been quick to realize that talking about suicide would cause others to restrict his freedom in the interests of safety. He adjusted his behavior accordingly. Even on Jane Brown 5 South, when he had a guitar in his hands, he seemed completely calm and recovered. Both John and Darla felt a sense of relief that this episode was behind them; Josh was himself again and would be released despite the uncomfortable family meeting. Their family would be restored.

Just before he was released, Josh asked his mother to buy a portable CD player as a gift for the young man who had been carrying around a broken one for the entire week. Darla picked out a bright red player, and she also brought a large package of assorted color pencils for the shy older man who liked to draw. Josh had developed a tremendous amount of empathy for these two people in particular during his stay, and he wanted to add some small pleasure to their lives.

A voluntary partial-hospitalization program was available for Josh to attend on a day-to-day basis, but he wanted no part of it. He was released after spending both his father's and his sister's birthdays in crisis or recovering from it. He would be home in time for his own thirtieth birthday.

Josh's diagnosis of "296.33 Major Depressive Disorder, Recurrent, Severe Without Psychotic Features" is both specific and vast. Families all across the country are dealing with depression on a daily basis. A National Center for Health Statistics, October 2011, Data Brief states, "Eleven percent of Americans aged 12 years and over take antidepressant medication." There are many interpretations of what is driving this trend in medication. Simple availability of antidepressants, along with the need of pharmaceutical companies to recover research costs and make a profit are sometimes cited as contributing to such numbers. It costs hundreds of millions of dollars to bring a new drug to market. In addition, direct-to-consumer advertising has changed the landscape of awareness.

Much is still unknown about the underlying reasons why so many people feel incapacitating episodes of emptiness, guilt, loss of pleasure, and hopelessness leading them to feel the need to elevate mood with psychoactive substances (either prescribed or illegal). In a January 23, 2012, story on National Public Radio, reporter Alix

Spiegel turned to experts to explore current thinking about causes and treatments for depression. A very popular narrative has been that depression is caused by low levels of serotonin, but this is now disputed. "Chemical imbalance is sort of last-century thinking. It's much more complicated than that," said Dr. Joseph Coyle, a professor of neuroscience at Harvard Medical School . . . "Scientific thinking has clearly shifted . . . while low serotonin probably doesn't cause depression, some abnormality in the serotonin system clearly plays a role. But most researchers have moved on," he continued, "and are looking at more fundamental issues like identifying the genes that might put people at risk for developing depression."

Spiegel's NPR piece, "When It Comes To Depression, Serotonin Isn't The Whole Story," concludes, "Unfortunately, the real story is complicated and, in a way, not all that reassuring. Researchers don't really know what causes depression. They're making progress, but they don't know."

Uncertainty about what causes depression is not going to help relieve stress and anxiety, and a great many people do find relief with one or more of the traditional chemical treatments. In addition, cognitive behavioral therapy (CBT) has shown remarkable results. According to the National Alliance on Mental Illness (NAMI), CBT offers "an empirically supported treatment that focuses on patterns of thinking that are maladaptive and the beliefs that underlie such thinking." A 2005 study in the Archives of General Psychiatry states, "Cognitive therapy can be as effective as medications for the initial treatment of moderate to severe major depression." Josh's treatments included both the chemical and the CBT options.

By the spring of 2010, Josh had prescriptions for a portfolio of psychopharmaceuticals to address various conditions. He had available all of the following, according to his medical records: Adderall for attention deficit hyperactivity disorder (ADHD), Abilify for mood augmentation, and Zoloft for depression. In addition, he was taking a sleep medication to help with insomnia and was offered Ativan as needed for anxiety. There is never any guarantee of a patient's compliance with recommended schedules of taking any or all of these. Josh had always been very intelligent but also fiercely independent and strategic. Drug prescriptions and recommendations for therapy are documented by hospital medical records and discharge documents, but a patient's subsequent actions and long-term follow-up are not. No one really monitored whether Josh was rigorous or casual in taking his medications after he was out of the hospital. Nor is it possible to know how genuine and faithful he was with the cognitive behavior therapy that was suggested.

In discussions with his physicians and therapists, Josh was also encouraged to continue creative outlets such as painting, music, and writing to help him process some of his feelings and their effects. Many of his lyrics, journal entries, and paintings are not dated. Like many people, he seemed to write more when he was experiencing troubling emotions, going through a tough break-up with a girl, or questioning his goals. When he uses names in a song lyric, poem, or journal entry, the feelings can be linked to a specific relationship and time.

Some of Josh's paintings from different periods of his life reveal the diversity of his experience and his feelings. He painted memorials to several of the music legends he admired: Stevie Ray Vaughan (1954-1990) and Jimi Hendrix (1942-1970). These paintings demonstrate his skills and vision as an artist. They are not whimsical and joyful, nor are they filled with any particular personal anguish even in their muted colors. Another painting—a twilight view of Stafford Pond near one of his homes in his twenties—portrays a serene landscape that seems to reflect a peaceful artist looking at a scene that confirms his positive view of the world.

The Stafford Pond painting contrasts most starkly with two self-portraits created in 2010. One of the self-portraits is done in grays and blacks and gives the impression of a severed head with eyes closed, downward cast features, and wisps of paint (or blood) dripping from the head. It is skilled in a sketch-like, macabre style that conveys a very dark mood. The features seem empty as in death, rather than paused as in sleep. The other self-portrait, done in vivid reds, deep blues, black, and white, depicts a head, shoulders, and forearm view of Josh. He is leaning forward with his head supported on both sides by his hands which cover his ears. He appears prematurely aged with a bald, skeleton-like head. Tears stream from his eyes down both sides of his face and around a deep, scowling frown. Unlike the emotionally blank grey and black portrait, this one is dripping with feeling. The figure's complex grimace seems to speak of insupportable anguish and self-recrimination. The wide outer frame of red around the figure is broken with diagonal lines. Behind the lines and the color is a sketch of the same face with dark hair and smiling eyes and mouth. The dominant figure in the center draws attention away from the faint, almost disappearing figure behind the red paint.

These paintings show Josh's creativity in two stages: before the dark times and in the grip of his massive despair. At this point, he was not painting, or possibly not even imagining, any scenarios where a figure would break through turbulent storms into the light of a new day.

CHAPTER VII

Riding the Roller Coaster

Blues is easy to play, but hard to feel.
Jimi Hendrix

JOSH OFFICIALLY RETURNED TO WORK after the hospitalization in March, and there were good days that were encouraging in how normal they felt. On the other hand, there were days when he could not make it to Newport. There were also periods when he stopped communicating with everyone in his life. He could spend several full days in bed in a semi-conscious state, seeking sleep as an escape from the whole world. Darla was very concerned and, one day, she called his counselor who told her that Josh should not be left alone.

John and Darla drove to Bristol and knocked on Josh's door. He had been sleeping and when he came to the door, he was very angry. On the surface, it was annoyance that they had disrupted his sleep, but there was a look about him that wasn't typical of Josh, not even of a sleepy and irritated Josh. This was one of the occasions when his parents would wonder if they were seeing the influence of his cocktail of medications. It could be side effects, or it could be a mistaken dosage. It could even be that his particular brain chemistry responded differently than expected to a particular chemical. They didn't know, and they were fairly certain that the psychiatrist, who did little more than prescribe the medications, didn't either.

Josh wasn't quite shouting at them, but he was intensely angry. "Get out of my house! You have no right to be here!" Before he could turn and slam the door, Darla spoke up. "We aren't leaving unless we know that you are OK." Josh snapped back, "If you don't leave, I'm calling the police!"

There was a brief standoff at the front door, and then Josh turned and made the call. Of course, it was his property and he had every right to his privacy—except for the fact that his parents were frantic with worry that he was not safe. When the police arrived, they were crystal clear about the fact that Darla and John were trespassing and that they had to leave. Darla was sobbing as they got in the car and drove away.

A few weeks went by with little or no communication between Josh and his parents. He removed Darla from access to his Facebook page. If he was plotting a strategy at all, a key feature of that strategy was to distance himself from his family. When he replied to text messages, it was with one-word answers, abrupt to the point of being rude. He should have known that nothing would drive them away.

Josh could carry on relationships in one area of his life while closing down and becoming icy-cold in other areas. For the latter half of March, he shut out his parents, but was still communicating with and seeing his sister and a few of his friends. By the end of the month, he had softened slightly toward his parents. When he slammed into the next wall, they rushed to his side.

On April 1, 2010—April Fool's Day—Josh had a brief and relatively innocuous interaction with Angela. Later in the day, when he was in the car doing errands with Darla, he picked up his cell phone to continue their conversation. It did not go well, and he burst into an angry tirade. In his outburst, he shouted various remarks indicating that he couldn't take this anymore and he would *show her* by hanging himself. He held himself back from physical violence with his mother in the car but lost control when they got back to the house. He picked up a baseball bat and began to smash furniture.

It didn't take long for John to respond to a call from Darla, and he brought reinforcements. Ted, a friend and colleague of John's, lived near Josh, and John called him to come over immediately. As soon as they entered the house, Josh made moves to leave, but John was not going to let him out of his sight. John forcibly pulled the bat out of Josh's hands. "What is the matter with you, Josh? Snap out of it! Cut this bullshit and pull yourself together!"

The two men restrained him. They didn't want to hurt Josh, who was very strong, and they didn't want to be injured themselves. John and Ted wrestled him to the ground. It was a titanic struggle between full-grown men exerting complete muscular strength and yet holding back any blow that might truly harm anyone. Finally, Josh quieted, and the older men backed off. He was furious with his father and neighbor for keeping him from running off in his frantic and self-destructive state. Even without bruises or blood, this kind of conflict can leave permanent scars. In this case, a measure of forgiveness softened the trauma. Several days afterward, in a quieter mood, Josh thanked his father for not letting him carry out his plans.

In the frantic moments of the struggle, however, Darla had called 911, and soon police and an ambulance arrived. There was nothing simple about the situation, and everyone did their best to balance safety with safeguarding rights. The police separated and secured Josh and brought him for an evaluation. After this due diligence and the determination that he was not a risk to himself or anyone else, they drove him home. Darla and John were still there, and they were vigorous and persuasive in voicing their fears for his immediate safety. Josh's outburst in the car and the destructive explosion back at the house had impressed Darla with the certainty that he was capable of violence to himself and that he was in urgent danger. The balancing act was now swinging in her favor. On his own, Josh was extremely persuasive, but in the presence of his parents, the system had to give full weight to their concerns and move in the direction of minimizing risk. The police transported him to Rhode Island Hospital Emergency Department for involuntary certification to Butler Hospital.

It was April 2nd by the time Josh was admitted at Butler Hospital. This facility in Providence, Rhode Island, is a well-known and well-respected psychiatric hospital treating children, adolescents, and adults. It is affiliated with the Warren Alpert Medical School of Brown University. Upon admission, Josh was interviewed, though quite reluctantly. He commented that he did not belong in the hospital at all and that he did not want any contact with his parents at any time during his hospitalization. He denied any suicidal or homicidal intentions, as well as stating that he had no delusions, mania, or post-traumatic stress disorder, and no history of violence, financial or legal problems, or drug abuse. He stated that the break-up with his ex-girlfriend was the recurring source of his stress, even though it had occurred months and months before.

The physician assigned to Josh's case was Dr. Richard Charles. This was perhaps the most fortunate pairing of patient and provider in his entire life. The two men were similar in age, and they formed a bond based on communication and trust. Dr. Charles was consistent in his daily visits with Josh and daily phone calls to Maggie with updates. He took the time to listen carefully, and Josh felt that Dr. Charles understood the various complications of his whole story and that he genuinely cared about what would happen next. Josh could talk to Dr. Charles about a family history of depression and medications and about his own history of episodes of depression, anxiety, and anger beginning as far back as junior high school. He could also talk about his new puppy, a sure sign of future-oriented thinking.

During the first week of his stay, he had admitted to Dr. Charles that if he hadn't been admitted, he might have taken his own life. He also spoke to a nurse about being safe while in the hospital but that he was still considering death as a way to make his problems go away. After several requests by Dr. Charles, Josh signed releases allowing the physician to call Darla, John, and Maggie. Maggie felt this was a good sign—that Josh was willing to let his doctor find out the facts about his life and his problems. If Dr. Charles could assemble and study all the malfunctioning parts, then there was a better chance that he could oversee an effective treatment.

Dr. Charles learned that, at an earlier time of crisis in his relationship with Angela, Josh had threatened to kill himself. Apparently, they were arguing out of doors, and Josh had handed her a knife. When she refused to harm him, he took the knife and gestured as if he were going to cut himself. Dr. Charles understood that the relationship was completely over and that Josh's persistent efforts to contact her were not welcome. John revealed to Dr. Charles that he had removed firearms from Josh's house as a precautionary measure.

In general, Josh was not willing to talk much to other staff, but on April 6th, he opened up to one of the nurses about his feelings. "I dated someone for 5 years, and I guess I was controlling, but I didn't want her to go out with her friends to the club because all the guys drool over them and I don't trust her friends. So I was stupid and broke up with her, thinking she would come back to me and she didn't . . . This girl is my soul mate and best friend . . . She is the one for me, and I can't get over her."

This nurse and many, many others oriented their therapeutic exchanges with Josh toward the cognitive coping skills of understanding his own behavior and revising his vision of the future. A treatment plan was gradually developed to help Josh cope with future episodes. He should take his medications as prescribed, avoid alcohol, keep all of his follow-up appointments, and follow his safety plan if suicidal thoughts were to recur. Dr. Charles gave him concrete suggestions of what to do when he got into a horrible state of panic or overwhelming sadness. In addition to activating other strategies and resources, he encouraged Josh to paint and to write when he got upset.

Toward the end of his involuntary commitment, Dr. Charles assessed Josh's state of mind and found him much improved in mood and sociability from the date of his admission and stable enough for release. He was well-groomed and talked about looking forward to being with his puppy and to returning to work. Despite these good signs, his rigid coping style was noted, along with poor decision-making skills and a habit of demanding immediate gratification of his needs. Josh was not quite released: he was transferred to the partial hospitalization program (PHP) with comments of "Substantial risk of decompensation" (worsening of symptoms) and "longstanding pattern of use of suicidality when confronted with issues of relationship termination." A "Progress Note" regarding his PHP admission states that his physician told him that, if he didn't continue his care in the PHP, a court order would be sought mandating further treatment.

Josh participated in a session or two on the first day of his admission to the partial hospitalization program. Mostly, he made clear to anyone he spoke with that, in his view, "This is a big waste of time. Honestly, I don't intend to participate in any of this."

He returned on the second day and insisted that he was improved and was not going to attend further. Dr. Charles and a social worker spent an hour with him and concluded that he could be discharged. Everyone agreed that he was more hopeful and flexible in his thought processes, and that he had already shown signs of picking up his normal routines and family relationships. He scheduled a follow-up outpatient appointment for the following week and was discharged on April 14, 2010.

Ups and Downs

Depending on the day that spring, Josh was either doing fine or he was partly impaired by his fixation on the loss of his ideal future and all the feelings that went along with that. He was seeing a psychiatrist once or twice a month and a therapist once a week. He was staying in contact with his family, and he even returned to work for a few weeks. He was open to possibly finding a new romantic relationship. Putting one foot in front of the other to maintain simple functioning is not quite the same as flourishing, however. Josh was going through the motions, at times with enough vitality to be really persuasive about his well-being, but at other times revealing the depth of his pain.

Melissa Ceprano, his good friend from work, became aware of these complexities in early May, when they made plans to get together. She went to Bristol on May 5, 2010, to meet Josh's new puppy, Austin. "Since it was El Cinco de Mayo, he greeted me with a margarita. We ended up heading down the street to Wharfside, a local bar, for dinner and more margaritas. We talked all night."

The two friends hadn't seen one another in quite a while. Melissa had recently gotten married, and Josh had been working on and off since sometime in March. She noticed that his attitude had morphed from mostly positive to being very bitter about everything. "Everything we talked about, he had something negative to say about it. He told me that his bitterness was stemming from his recent breakup with his ex-girlfriend. The truth started to come out, and I became very concerned for my friend."

That night, Josh also told Melissa about his hospitalization at Butler. She put two and two together and realized that this was why he had been away from work for so long. A generous woman with her own lively spirit, Melissa brought out the fun-loving Josh, and together they laughed through hours and hours that would otherwise have been grim and empty. On other visits, they watched TV and played video games together, giggling like kids at the lines that tickled them, like "I want to spray hot hug all over you" from *Family Guy*. They had countless meals together at Jacky's Galaxie, became addicted together to Nim Chow, and amassed a huge collection of fortune cookies. They had tons of fun trying and failing to train Austin, possibly more fun than succeeding. Austin was a perfect foil for all sorts of entertainment; they renamed him "Glen" for a day and got a charge out of his confusion and the odd sound of the name on their lips.

Sometimes, the day would lead them in a direction that revealed a little more of Josh's despondent moods. Melissa was sensitive to this and could connect with him in these moods, too. "The day he played the song 'She Talked to Angels' by Black Crows on his guitar, I ended up crying because he sounded so good."

Josh could bring out these feelings in his friend because he was playing the song from deep in his own heart: a compelling woman slipping away and the "pain [that's] gonna make everything all right." They could go from intense moments like this to hours of hanging out on the deck in 95-degree weather, trying to name all the states and capitals or watching a movie like *The Ringer* and laughing their heads off. More than anyone else, Melissa could lift his spirits and help him get through the days and nights that sometimes felt unbearable.

The first few weeks of May went fairly well. Josh was working and having an occasional date. He was communicating with the family. The only issue he was having was balancing his medications so that his mood was maximized and side effects were minimized. He wasn't happy with the side effects of one medication, so he decreased the dosage on his own. It seems like a small thing, but it can have disturbing consequences. For Josh, the consequences were "brain zaps" that felt like a lightning storm was trapped inside his head. He called his father from work one day and asked him to come and take him to the doctor. He was confused and scared about the intense symptoms. "I don't know what's wrong with me. I can't explain it; it's like my brain just isn't right!" Josh was advised to restart the medication at a lower dose.

It was in about the third week of May that Josh was derailed by another emotional crisis. Angela was graduating from her nursing program, and he was absolutely distraught that he was never going to celebrate an event like this with her and the boys. It was not going to be a milestone in their life together, the way they had planned long ago. He forced himself to put on a good face and to attend a

Memorial Day picnic, but when he had to go home alone yet again, he allowed the downward spiral to take over. He went to bed and missed several days of work. He stopped answering text messages and the phone.

After three days of not hearing from Josh, his parents went to his house. Josh was asleep when they arrived, but he roused himself to demand that they leave. They refused to leave and based on his condition, they called the police. Josh's rights to privacy and to choose when to function or not to function according to conventional standards were overruled by his parents' concerns for his safety. His history of suicide intentions was also weighed against him. The police consulted with his outpatient psychiatrist and then transported him, in handcuffs, to Rhode Island Hospital for evaluation. He was admitted to Butler Hospital again the following day, June 3rd.

Fortunately, Josh was again in the care of Dr. Richard Charles, who could see that he was "markedly different from previous admission." In fact, Dr. Charles noted that this admission appeared to be "largely driven by poor communication between the patient and his parents." Their sessions together were "focused on addressing cognitive distortions of all/nothing thinking." By June 8th, Josh was showing improved mood and greater ability to rely on the cognitive behavioral therapy strategies that he had been coached to use. He seemed more hopeful and clearly understood the benefits of the resources offered to him as an outpatient. His occasional irritability was noted, but this was offset by his general good mood and future-oriented goals.

He was discharged on June 8th, but he was not ready to forgive his parents for their role in putting him back in the hospital.

A Quiet Father's Day

Jamestown, Rhode Island, is an idyllic locale all year round, and even more so on a beautiful June day. Father's Day, June 20, 2010, started out as a fair weather day in Jamestown, but there were at least three hearts heavy with storms passing through. On a typical Father's Day, John would have a card from Josh. One of his favorites showed a man and a boy following a dog across a field. It said, "For a Wonderful Dad, with Love and Thanks on Father's Day." Josh had double-underlined several phrases on the inside of the card: "You've been someone to lean on, to <u>learn from</u>, and to <u>look up to</u>. Thank you for being a father, a teacher, a friend . . . and so much more." He had signed it with love, but John's favorite touch was that Josh had sketched fishing poles in the hands of both the man and the boy on the front of the card. That card spoke of better days.

Maggie Barber roused herself to try to lift the dark cloud surrounding their family and create a small safe space to celebrate Father's Day 2010. Maggie, Darla, and John had been living on a roller coaster of sorts with Josh's frequent episodes of acute anxiety, depression, and suicidal intentions. Between one crisis and the next, they still believed he was at *the* turning point when life would resume its comfortable shape of more than a year ago. Today, however, after many conflicts over his safety and their actions, Josh did not want to see or talk to his parents. There was no negotiating his position; he was capable of screaming at them and reporting them to the police for trespassing. Josh and Maggie were still in close contact, often talking or texting daily. Despite Maggie's pleading, he refused to visit his parents on Father's Day, leaving the three of them alone, although Josh was always with them, deeply lodged in mind, heart, and spirit. On days like this, he seemed to inhabit their very arms and legs, making it difficult to move even from a chair to the car.

"Let's try to make the best of this day," said Maggie, making the effort for her father's sake. "Yes!" Darla picked up on her daughter's call for an energetic action to break the mood. "We'll get some sandwiches at Ace's and go out on the boat for a few hours. It looks like the perfect day for it." Mostly to humor his wife and daughter, John gruffly agreed. "OK, if you want to go, we'll go."

Picking up keys, wallets, and caps; changing from sandals into boat shoes and grabbing an extra shirt—this little bit of activity shifted currents in the air around the three of them and made it easier to breathe. They felt a tad bit better about their ability to walk away from Josh's problems to live their own separate lives, even for a few hours, and to respect his wishes to be left alone.

John drove the pick-up to Ace's and as they pulled into the parking lot, out of habit, they recited their sandwich orders. Their shows of appetite were more for moral support than for nutrition or actual hunger at this moment, though pretending also has its own demands for satisfaction.

Fortified, they drove to the boatyard at Fort Wetherill State Park. As they pulled into the parking lot, it was difficult not to notice that a blanket of fog was simultaneously pulling in to swallow all the boats. "We're totally socked in!" John exclaimed, hitting the steering wheel with his fist. Maggie and Darla could guess what he was thinking, "Can't we get even a little break today?" and they diverted their own disappointment into a suggestion that they all just go home, eat their sandwiches out on the deck, and have a relaxing afternoon. "It wouldn't be any fun to try to go out in this!" interjected Darla. "We'll just hang out together on the deck, and it will be a nice afternoon. Come on, let's go!"

They drove home in silence, each processing what it meant that their plans to step off the island and onto the sea had been thwarted. More than one of them was thinking, *That fog is some kind of a sign, isn't it?*

Back at the house by about 1 PM, they brought the sandwiches out to the deck overlooking the west passage of Narragansett Bay. Here there was no fog, no sign that their plans had been foiled. From the deck of the Barber house, it is a peaceful view down a wooded hillside with a few visible rooftops to the broad blue water of the bay and Quonset Point in the distance. Of all the rooms in their home, this deck of open air walls and blue sky ceiling was the true *family room* where they were most secure and at ease.

John's cell phone rang. He answered it, listened for a second, and then said, "Josh, are you all right?" in a voice filled with alarm. "Let me talk to Maggie!" was the urgent reply.

Father's Day Crisis for Josh

Josh woke up late on the Sunday morning of Father's Day, June 20, 2010. He couldn't entirely shake that foggy hangover feeling he had almost every morning, but today he had a little more energy than most days. He picked up his Fender Strat almost before his eyes were open; the fingerings still came easily, along with sounds that soothed him to a semi-awake state. He didn't know if he could get up even one more day if this was taken away. The guitar and Austin were about the only things that roused him even this much.

It was almost noon by the time Josh and Austin headed for Colt State Park, not far from home in Bristol, for a walk. This park was a favorite destination for Josh. Located along Narragansett Bay, Colt State Park is a refuge of quiet shady trails, acres of lawns and trees, beaches, and picnic groves. He could loosen up a little there and let his mind rest in the uncomplicated calm, although he did try to avoid focusing on the cheerful family groups lounging on blankets or tossing a Frisbee.

On this day, one family group on the beach caught his attention: a petite blonde woman, two active boys about the right ages, and a familiar masculine figure. His instantaneous response was to turn away, but in that split second, it was already too late. He was riveted, rooted to the ground with a blur of black fur spinning around his ankles. In that way that persuades us that our eye beams are actually microscopic particles hitting the person we see, Jason turned around, saw Josh, and shifted his weight to run toward him. He had actually broken out into a big smile and taken a couple of steps toward Josh when, behind him, his mother said a few words. The boy stopped, dropped his eyes, and turned away. Angela had also seen Josh and

Austin, and, clearly, she was not going to allow any contact between him and her sons.

How can the same exact revelation cause such extreme pain each time as if for the first time? Josh wasn't quite capable of framing such a coherent thought as Jason turned away, but he did feel a crushing blow that seemed to obliterate daylight along with every little blade of the grass that had cushioned his steps.

Was it by chance that Angela and her brother Adam, along with her two boys, Jason and Nick, had also decided to enjoy a few hours on Father's Day at Colt State Park? They knew that Josh went there often. Josh and Adam had developed a friendship over the four years of Josh and Angela's relationship. They hung out together, laughed, barbecued, had beers, and punched each other's shoulders; they were friends. As Josh walked back to his car alone with Austin, a little while after the incident, he encountered Adam in the parking lot. "I saw them." Josh said in a flat tone from the empty space left inside his chest. Adam couldn't say anything in response to this statement, but he nodded his head slightly. "I saw the boys, and I'd really like to spend a little time with them, but I kind of feel like I shouldn't." Again, Adam's body agreed with Josh, but this time, his shoulders acknowledged the love and the pain in Josh's words. Two beats later, he spoke. "Yeah, you probably shouldn't."

Josh got in the car and mechanically drove the short distance home with Austin. Then he allowed the shock and panic to take over.

It all happened so quickly; he wasn't even thinking. He was riding a devastating wave of emotion from the encounter at the park. He had just seen a demonstration of how well Angela and the boys were doing without him. They were going on with their lives, making plans, being happy, having fun, and he was *nothing* to them, less than nothing. He could never reach out and touch them again. Cymbals were crashing somewhere, the eerie silence and immanent violence of a tornado was suffocating him, large window panes were shattering inside his head. In a sudden burst of frenzy, Josh ripped the high definition cable out of the back of his television set. With single-minded purpose, he threw the cable over an exposed beam and fashioned the noose that would be his escape from this extreme pain.

Mobilizing Assistance

Maggie took the phone from her father's hands and put it to her ear. Josh was sobbing so hard that it was difficult to understand what he was saying. She recognized that he was in an extreme state of anxiety. He had tried calling Maggie's cell phone—which she had left in the house—then his parents' house phone, and finally, desperate to find his sister, he called his father's cell phone and demanded to speak to Maggie. "Where are you?" Josh finally calmed himself enough to ask. "I'm at Mom's and Dad's in Jamestown," Maggie replied. Josh sobbed, "Can you come over here?"

At Josh's request, Maggie immediately sprang into action. He almost never asked her to come to him; she sensed the urgency of the request at once, and she picked up her things and headed for the door. On her way out, she turned to John and said, "I'm sorry, Dad. I wanted this day to be about you. I love you."

Maggie got in her car for the familiar forty minute drive from Jamestown to Bristol, and they talked as she drove. "I'm coming now! What's the matter?" Mostly, it was Maggie trying to calm Josh enough so that he could speak coherently and tell her what was going on. "It's all right. It's going to be all right," Maggie repeated over and over again. "You called me, and I'm coming to help you. I'm on my way."

Maggie was alone in the car, and she felt quite isolated with the current situation, whatever it was. Josh refused to have his parents near him, and the past few months of inpatient and outpatient experiences had left the entire family exhausted and disillusioned with a mental health system that couldn't or wouldn't find a successful healing process for Josh.

"Don't call the police! I don't want you to call the police!"

Maggie couldn't understand why Josh was fixated on this. "Why would I call the police? You called me looking for my help, and I'm coming to help you. I'm coming by myself. I'll be there soon. It's going to be all right. Why don't you take your Xanax?"

By about the halfway point in the drive, Maggie was able to glean a few facts from Josh and realized why he was so insistent that she not call the police. Through his sobs, Josh managed to tell his sister that he had tried to kill himself.

Maggie Barber was twenty-seven years old at this time. She was and is a trained occupational therapist with a background in social work. She knew she must stay on the phone with her brother and keep him talking. There is no small amount of courage involved in driving steadfastly toward such a situation while brainstorming possible options and keeping your own emotions under control. She asked Josh to tell her what happened.

He could barely get the words out through the sobbing. "I hung myself . . . it broke and I woke up . . . scrambling on the floor . . . if it didn't break, I wouldn't be here anymore. It would all be over."

Maggie knew that Josh was saying he wished it *was* over. Shifting gears mentally, she admitted to herself that this was a much more serious incident than ever before. She told Josh that this time, it was more than she could handle alone. "This is bigger than me. You asked for my help, but I can't help you on my own this time. I'm right down the road and I'll be there in a minute. Right now I need you to think about what we're going to do next." And then Maggie hung up and called their parents. She could picture Darla and John at home in a state of total anxiety, not knowing what new crisis their son was going through and whether they could do anything at all. For no more than thirty seconds, she filled them in on what Josh had just told her, and then she pulled into Josh's driveway and got out of the car. Maggie turned her complete attention to what she would face on the other side of the front door.

Josh was sitting on the couch with his head in his hands, sobbing. The stepladder was still there, and the cable was still hanging from the open beam in the living room. There were raw red marks around his neck, and he couldn't stop sobbing and coughing and gagging.

Maggie was struggling to keep herself calm, though she felt on the verge of losing control. She didn't cry but just sat beside Josh, rubbing his back, and saying over and over, "It's all right. It's going to be all right." Meanwhile, she was trying to figure out what she was going to do.

It was clear to Maggie from her observations of the room that this was not an intentionally failed or faked suicide attempt. She didn't believe for one second that Josh wanted that cable to break. He wasn't one to screw anything up. He had hung long enough to lose consciousness, and when the cable broke, he had fallen onto Austin's metal crate and smashed it.

Maggie finally decided that she either had to get him to go with her for help, or she would have to call 911. "Why don't you take a ride with me, and we'll drive by Butler, and we'll see if Dr. Charles is around? We'll see if you can talk to him."

"No! I don't want this anymore. I don't want any help; I don't want to talk to anybody. It's over. I don't want anybody's help."

She tried to persuade him once again, talking calmly and firmly. Josh refused and refused. Maggie gave him an ultimatum. "I need you to come with me, or I'm going to call the police to take you to the hospital." He mumbled about "the dungeon," and Maggie assured him that she would stay with him through every moment. They were both thinking about the dark basement at Rhode Island Hospital where patients are stored while waiting for psychiatric evaluation. "What if they won't let you stay with me?" Maggie replied, "Then I won't let them take you!"

It broke Maggie's heart to see her big brother more vulnerable and desperate than ever before. She had been with Josh for many of the horrors of previous hospital experiences. Because he had called her when he regained consciousness, she reasoned, he must have wanted her help. The situation was overwhelming her, and the best help she could give her brother was to involve others. She wanted to believe that if she was by his side as his advocate, she could ensure that it wouldn't be such a painful process this time. She kept saying, "This is bigger than me. You called me for my help. I can't help you through this on my own."

Josh just sat on the sofa, crying and not saying anything. Maggie had the phone in her hand, and she pressured him for a response. She already had the number to the Bristol police department in her phone. "Josh, if you don't get in the car and let me drive you to the hospital, I'm going to call the rescue number. Will you come with me now?" Josh said, "No," and she made the call. There was no anger left in him this time. All of the other times, he had railed against them for calling the police. This time he was empty, at the very bottom of his reserves with nothing left, just tears.

The ambulance came, and after Maggie and Josh answered all of their questions, they took Josh's vital signs and walked him out to the vehicle. Maggie climbed in with them. Josh wasn't quite there, and Maggie was feeling a tremendous rush of anxiety. With sirens blaring, they drove away to Rhode Island Hospital.

The Dungeon

The wait was agonizing. Josh was barely aware of the activity surging around them. His emotions had peaked hours before, and he was now quite subdued, almost catatonic. Maggie was channeling all of her energy into reassuring Josh and trying to ease the process along by making sure they were not overlooked in the chaos. After hours in the ER, where he got x-rays of his cervical spine and IV fluids, he was moved downstairs to "D-Pod." This was the worst—the "dungeon" he had particularly wanted to avoid. It was a unit of tiny stalls underground. No windows, no privacy, bright lights, drunk people stumbling out of their stalls with guards corralling them back in, and the few unfortunates who fulfilled every stereotype of crazy that you might see on TV.

Maggie was determined to make the experience better in some way. She requested anxiety medication for her brother and would periodically ask a nurse for an update on next steps, hoping that merely by asking she could speed up the process. She also called Butler Hospital to find out if there was a bed for Josh when it became official that he needed to be admitted. All in all, as both Maggie and Josh realized later, there might have been some minuscule effect of her advocacy, but it wasn't much. Perhaps for some VIP in crisis, there was swift and comfortable treatment, but for almost everyone else, the system was the system—sluggish and impersonal, a big shoebox of a system, pushed under the bed where you throw odds and ends because they don't fit in the custom-made, velvet-covered boxes. Imagine a labor, delivery, and maternity wing or a children's cancer hospital in a basement with tiny stalls all in a row. For some categories of clients, every hospital airs the best rooms and puts out the best linen. For Josh and the others on many psychiatric wards, containment—not healing, and certainly not a comforting atmosphere—is the first priority.

Before Josh said "No," and Maggie catapulted both of them into the system with her phone call, she had sent a text message to Darla and John, letting them know that she would get Josh to a hospital. Her mission was to get him through the system at Rhode Island Hospital and, if he needed to be admitted, to get him admitted at Butler Hospital, just a few miles across the city, but in her mind, eons away from the horrors Josh had experienced on the inpatient psychiatric ward at Rhode Island Hospital.

Sleeping through the night is not an option in *the dungeon*. Josh would nod off from time to time for a few moments, but Maggie was alert and sensitive to every shriek, every odor, every wave of urgency sweeping through the unit. Every couple of hours—hundreds of minutes, thousands of seconds—a nurse might stop by with a brief glance of concern, and Maggie would try to engage her or him to find out what might happen and when. Most often, they could tell her nothing and would move away to the next stall without even a smile of encouragement. Despite his overall distress, Josh seemed comforted by her presence and that was reason enough to stay awake by his side. Maggie, like her mother, is short in stature but formidable when protecting her family.

After the long night, the transport team arrived at Josh's stall without any advance notice, and Maggie immediately insisted that she was coming along in the ambulance. The wait for admission at Butler was another couple of hours, but at least the environment was a little better. Food was available in the waiting area in acknowledgment that some people would be there for many hours. A seventeen-year-old girl in a manic state was shaking and fluttering around the room, swearing viciously at her mother when not talking a blue streak to no one in particular. Although it was a partial distraction, this display did nothing to soothe anyone else in the room.

Now that they were at Butler, Maggie moved on to her next mission: seeing to it that her brother would be assigned to the care of Dr. Richard Charles whom Josh trusted from his previous stay at Butler. She had already called and determined that there was a bed available on his floor. Not much was going their way, but it really seemed that this would work out. The admitting physician said, "I don't see any reason why that wouldn't be possible. You should be fine."

Maggie stayed by Josh's side until he was brought up to the unit on D-4. It wasn't visiting hours and she had to leave. She hugged him and promised to call and come back as soon as it was permitted. Maggie left and Josh entered the unit with a nurse.

Josh had been having both interior and actual conversations about ending his life for some months by the time of this failed attempt. It was an active debate, but occasionally he built enough clarity and volition to tip him in one direction or the other. A similar ambivalence was true for his immediate family and friends; many days they felt sure the worst was behind them, but on Josh's darkest days, they felt on the edge of losing him entirely.

In early March, Josh had written long letters to Angela's two sons, expressing his love as well as his apologies for some of the arguments they had witnessed between him and their mother. The letters deliver serious and complex messages from someone who was a father figure in their lives for over four years. He linked back to fun times, encouraged them to love and respect their mother, expressed his love and hopes for them, and admitted to his own failings along with his efforts to be a better person.

> *Although I know I could've done better with/for you both I did the best I could at the time . . . Just like you used to take a pill for ADD, I take one for depression and anxiety. Anxiety can be like panic attacks or general agitation. So I went almost 30 years of my life being like that . . . and it sucked. Depression is hard to deal with, and I'm so much more stable of a person now as a result of that and talking to a counselor. I want you both to know, you both have always been great kids, and I over-reacted many times about things. I'll always regret that for the rest of my life . . . just as I regret not handling things with your Mom differently.*

On the surface the letters are a farewell due to the break-up of the relationship between Josh and Angela, but given the timing and the tone of the letters, they seem even more final than this. Josh ends the letters with a promise to "be there for you both," which reaches out into a hopeful and positive future even as he says a final "Good-bye."

There were so many times when his suicidal intentions came close to the surface. At one point during the early summer, Josh had bought a book for his mother. Darla took one look at the title—*Healing After the Suicide of a Loved One*—and refused to read it. Josh was sending messages to his family through actions that showed his love and concern for them. Darla was much more receptive to people who would try to console her with folk wisdom like, "When people talk about suicide openly, they're really *not* going to do it." She was, of course, hoping that was true. But she also sensed how deep Josh's pain was. Other people didn't know because they weren't with him every day. "We knew the seriousness of it, and we knew that it *could* happen, but Father's Day was when we realized it was *really* real. When he actually did it, even though he failed, we finally believed he would make the attempt."

Within the System

Even though the admitting doctor at Butler didn't see any reason why Josh would not be assigned to Dr. Charles again, there was someone higher up who did not agree. Josh's family could not believe that, after all of their advocacy for Dr. Charles, Josh could have been randomly assigned to a different doctor. It must have been deliberate. Despite being told that this was not the case, Maggie could see that there was a certain logic to the decision. "I'm sure that they met as a team and said, 'something's not working,' so they assigned him to a different doctor. I don't know whether it was protocol or not, but I think because he had seen Dr. Charles twice, and was discharged twice, and then hung himself, they weren't giving him to the same doctor again. I don't think for one minute that it was Dr. Charles's decision."

After Maggie left Josh at Butler on that Monday morning, he slept deeply for most of the day. At some point during the day, Noah Philip came into the room and woke him up. At first, Josh was relieved to see the familiar face of his trusted doctor. Then he listened to what Dr. Charles was saying. "Josh, I just want to let you know that I'm not going to be your doctor this time. I'm really sorry."

Josh was still groggy from the emotional and physical trauma of the day before and from the nearly sleepless night in emergency rooms. He heard these words and then drifted back to sleep. The meaning incubated for a few hours, and when he finally woke to full consciousness, he was angry along with having a strong sense of dread for the coming days.

The adult psychiatric ward on D-4 was very different from the one at Rhode Island Hospital. Many of the other patients here were similar to Josh in that they seemed to be suffering from acute issues that didn't completely obscure their intelligence and functioning. In the eyes of his family members, Josh was hospitalized for self-protection and to identify strategies to treat his depression. Even here, the other patients would have combative outbursts and sometimes would have to be restrained or sedated. This was not the case with Josh, who, after his episode, seemed quite normal to his family. They observed that, in some settings, patients with symptoms as diverse as depression and severe mental illness were treated similarly, often to the detriment of both.

Josh woke up angry that he would not be treated by Dr. Charles. He saw Dr. Charles almost daily, talking to other patients on the floor. Dr. Charles knew his story, and Josh felt respected and understood in his care. This was not the case with the physician assigned to his case this time. Possibly she sensed her new patient's feelings on the matter; there was no doubt that the two of them got off on the wrong foot. Josh resented having to tell his history over again to a new doctor. He did not feel any empathy from her; in fact, he felt a certain hostility that came across in remarks that he found condescending. His reaction to this was an attitude of merely tolerating her presence. He had no interest in cooperating with someone who appeared not to respect him. Speaking from his own experience, writer Andrew Solomon suggests that "People you dislike, no matter how skilled they are, cannot help you."

Because Butler is a teaching hospital, the physician on his case brought students into Josh's room when she visited him. Josh found it difficult to talk about his life with young medical students listening and taking notes. He surmised that these novices would discuss his case, and the very thought appalled him. "I'm tired of telling the story over and over again. I don't want to be their lesson. I'm not interested in having them take notes on my heartache."

Maggie coached Josh on how to courteously state his preference that students not participate in his treatment. He made the request to his doctor, and she never again brought students into his room, but there were repercussions. The nurses didn't seem to notice one way or the other, but when Josh casually asked a passing medical student a simple question about an ordinary hospital routine, the student replied rudely, "Oh, I'm not supposed to talk to you. I was told that I'm not to be involved in your care."

Rather than assuming that everyone on staff *always* behaves in a respectful and supportive manner to all patients, this student may have absorbed an attitude of resentment toward a patient who elected not to participate in some of the educational functions of the hospital. Josh felt that, although she complied with his wishes for greater privacy, the doctor also was passive-aggressive in her attitude toward him, making remarks that gave clear signals of her disdain for this decision. Josh was too sharp to miss the import of her comments, and yet, he was not about to act out his true feelings. His reaction was more likely to be a further deepening of resolve not to cooperate with her. None of this was helpful for his recovery. The two were locked in a subtle battle, neither of them with the freedom to withdraw. Once again, Josh felt captive to the mental health care system that his family had invoked to protect and help him.

Josh wasn't on speaking terms with his parents at this time; Maggie was the only one he was willing to see and talk to. The day after he was admitted, he confided in Maggie his thoughts on what he had done on the afternoon of Father's Day. "I know how easy it is now. It didn't even hurt. I just passed out, and that was it until the cord broke and I woke up on the floor. It was so easy."

Maggie was disturbed to hear her brother reveal these thoughts. If he had been frightened previously of what it might be like to die by hanging, he no longer was afraid. He knew exactly what it would be like, and he had concluded that "It was easy." Was he telling her intentionally as a precaution, to alert her to the need to be extra vigilant with him in future? Maggie couldn't tell precisely what his motives were, but she had a clear sense that the obstacles standing between Josh and grievous danger were evaporating.

The hospitalization period in June may not have been wholly therapeutic for Josh, but it was an effective safeguard against an immediate threat. The involuntary period for this admission was ten days. As with previous hospitalizations, Josh recovered his composure quickly enough to know what his rights were and what he needed to do in order to be released when the mandatory time period had elapsed.

In addition to daily visits, Maggie was also trying to keep informed of his condition and compliance. Over and above Josh's relationship with Dr. Richard Charles, Maggie had appreciated his daily phone calls with updates when Josh had been under his care at Butler. This time, however, she would make three or four calls to the hospital over several days to get even one response from a social worker or a nurse, but never from the doctor.

Maggie was aware, from Josh himself, that he was refusing to take an additional medication that had been prescribed for him. They both knew that the refusal could be viewed as non-compliance with his therapy. This could be a justification to take him to court for an extended commitment instead of releasing him. They differed on whether this was desirable. Josh wanted to be free, and Maggie was adamant that he not be released. She saw no improvement in his attitude; in fact, she was more concerned than ever about his intentions.

In decades gone by, an involuntary commitment after a failed suicide attempt might have been at least double or triple the amount of time that Josh was retained. For some patients, this may have proved more therapeutic with more time for medications to stabilize and for relationships to form with therapists offering beneficial strategies. More recently, an inpatient stay seems to serve primarily for crisis management and for evaluation, and the real work of readjusting attitudes and life patterns *must* be accomplished outside the hospital.

This change, however, was not accompanied by the creation of effective transition methods. The partial hospitalization program may have been designed for just this purpose, but Josh managed to slip through this version of a safety net.

John and Darla had gone to Butler several times during this episode to visit Josh, but he refused to see them. He was still angry and keeping his distance. One day Darla managed to get past the nurses' station. She saw Josh sitting alone playing his guitar in a sunny lounge area, and she started walking toward him. He didn't see her coming until she was about ten steps away. He quickly got up and went to get a nurse. "Tell her to leave! I don't want to see her!"

Darla thought about arguing, but she didn't want to make a scene. Nor could she speak with the huge lump in her throat. All she really wanted was a hug. It didn't seem to be too much to hope for, and she couldn't believe Josh would deny her this if he knew how much his refusal hurt. No words passed between mother and son, but Darla felt that someone had slipped a knife into her heart.

Toward the end of the ten days, Maggie had one phone call from the physician in preparation for possible scenarios. "If we get to the tenth day, and he's not willing to sign himself in, we will go to court."

Maggie was full of questions. "What does that mean? Does he go in person? Does he need a lawyer? What if the court says he can go home?" The doctor replied, "Then he walks out of the courthouse and goes home."

This conversation did nothing to calm Maggie's fears. She knew her brother would figure out a way to manage his release if the medical team did not have a preemptive strategy. Josh had already contacted an attorney who was a friend of the family, and he had informed Maggie that he would need her to bring his good suit to wear to court. If they took him to court, Josh would be in his best suit and on his best behavior—of completely sane mind and fully capable of making intelligent choices regarding his own life. The judge would have to release him.

Just before the deadline, however, without any notification to her patient or his family, Josh's doctor went on vacation. The covering doctor promised Maggie that the plan was still the same: they were not letting him go. They had not made any progress; he was not taking the medication that they wanted him to take; he wasn't going anywhere. They were encouraging him to sign himself into the hospital voluntarily, but if he didn't do so, they were going to take him to court.

Maggie tried to convince Josh that it probably would be in his best interest to start taking the medication that they wanted him to try. She felt it would be better for him to be compliant and sign himself in voluntarily than to receive a court-ordered mandate. But Josh had a game plan that he didn't share with his sister. He waited until the last minute, and on the very day that the court proceedings would be set in motion, he took the medication and signed himself in. The Barbers were momentarily relieved that Josh had recognized the need to have additional therapy in the hospital. And then they realized that if he had signed himself in voluntarily, he could also legally sign himself out. The covering doctor assured them, "Technically that is true, but actually, when you sign yourself out, all it means is that you are guaranteed an evaluation from the psychiatrist the next day. That person will then determine whether you go home or not."

Maggie asked the hard question. "OK. So, let's say he signs himself out tomorrow, and he's evaluated. Are you going to make him stay?" "Yes, of course! At this point, he is not ready to go home."

Within twenty-four hours, Maggie got a call at work from a social worker who told her that Josh had signed himself out and was being discharged. She should be there to pick him up at 2:00 PM. Maggie insisted on speaking with the covering doctor, and after several more calls, he came to the phone. "You told me that he was not safe to go home, that he was going to stay there no matter what." He replied, "Well, yes, that was when I spoke with you yesterday; however, he is being compliant now, and he's taking his medication, and he assures us that he is going to try our day treatment program."

Josh's plan had trumped his sister, two doctors, the court, and the system. He was a brilliant escape artist. Maggie knew he had no intention of attending the outpatient day program as he had promised. He had been vehement on this topic with her earlier, "I'm not doing that. I have no interest in spending all day talking to people about what makes me sad. It's not going to happen!"

Maggie felt a sense of rising panic. She had felt calm all week knowing that Josh was safe in the hospital, but now he was front and center of her consciousness, flashing red and blue lights like an ambulance speeding toward a wreck.

Nothing Has Changed

Leaving work early on Friday, July 2, 2010, Maggie drove to Butler Hospital to pick up her brother. Everywhere, other people were also getting out of work early for the 4th of July weekend. There was a sense of hustle and bustle on the roads. Maggie knew this also meant reduced services in all health care facilities as doctors, nurses, technicians, and others headed out to ocean beaches, neighborhood parks, and family backyards for holiday weekend traditions of picnics and fireworks.

Josh was standing outside the hospital with a white paper bag filled with his things. His guitar was beside him on the sidewalk. When Maggie pulled up, he put the guitar and bag in the back seat and got in the passenger seat. The charade was over. He had persuaded everyone except his family that he was in good shape, but now came the letdown into his *real* life. There was no need to project positive, healthful energy or to pretend any sort of compliance. He pulled the hood of his jacket up over his head and slouched down in the seat.

Josh made no effort at conversation, and they drove in silence. Maggie felt increasingly tense. She thought about taking him directly to his house in Bristol but decided to take a detour to Jamestown. Austin stayed with Darla and John each time Josh was in the hospital. By going to pick up Austin, she could achieve two purposes: having the dog with him might help lift Josh's spirits, and Darla and John would get a chance to see their son. Maggie presented the plan to Josh as entirely about the dog but mentioned that he might see his mother because she was probably at home. His only response was, "Whatever . . . but I'm not going in the house."

When they pulled into the driveway in Jamestown, Maggie refrained from insisting that he greet Darla and kept him focused on the practical: "It's your dog. He has toys and food and a crate. I'm not carrying all that out by myself. You need to come inside and help me." Josh entered the house with his hood up just long enough to get everything. Darla was glad to see him up and functioning. In the foyer by the front door, she approached to hug and kiss him. "I'm glad you're home." She couldn't keep the emotion out of her voice, but Josh made no response. Darla could have focused on this lack of expression, but it had been such a traumatic period for all of them. Just seeing Josh for a few minutes seemed like a small step in the right direction. Josh loaded the car with Austin and his gear and got inside.

Maggie drove Josh to the house in Bristol and helped him unload the car and carry his things into the house. Nothing was changed or cleaned up from the way they had left the house almost two weeks before. The pot that he was gagging into was still on the floor; the stepladder was positioned near the beam, the broken cords were lying there, along with all of the disarray from his fall. At first, Josh seemed paralyzed, clearly unprepared to resume any of the activities of a normal life. Both he and Maggie felt that the eleven or twelve days that had elapsed since Father's Day had changed absolutely nothing. They were back in the same setting, trapped with the same destructive emotions. In some ways, it was worse because they had both lost confidence in the potential for professional help. What had been traumatic the first time was now devastating to revisit.

Maggie had tickets to go to a Red Sox game that night with Justin, and she was looking for signs of how Josh might be if she left him alone. After a few minutes of paralysis, she could tell that Josh was trying hard to break the dark spell of being back at the very spot where it had all seemed too much to bear. He was trying to get things back in order, rousing himself to take the small steps of cleaning the kitchen, putting clothes in the laundry. He put some music on. All of this was encouraging to Maggie because there had been plenty of times in the past when he had made no effort to lift his darker moods. It was a sunny, pleasant day, and that seemed to be part of the affirmative push.

After an hour or so of assisting with the process of making the house hospitable, Maggie began to think she might leave. "Josh, I'm going to go. Do you think you're OK to be by yourself?"

"Yes. I don't need you. I'm fine. I'm fine."

She was hesitating at the door, reluctant to turn away from him. "What are you doing tomorrow? I'll call you in the morning, and we can do something together."

Josh had walked her to the door with his cell phone in his hand. The door was already open. "I think I'm going to go out. I'm going to do something, go grocery shopping or something productive." Then he looked down and asked his sister to stay in touch. "Could you just keep in contact with me through texting for a little while?"

Maggie was puzzled, "What do you mean?"

"I don't know, I'm a little worried. Just keep in contact with me. Just keep in touch. It's fine." Maggie heard the fear in his voice and she closed the door. "I'm not going anywhere."

Josh immediately back-tracked, saying, "You don't need to stay with me! I'm fine. Go wherever you're supposed to go!" But Maggie was firm. "I'm not going anywhere. What do you want for dinner? We'll just hang out." She stayed with him, and it wasn't long before the downward spiral began yet again.

Keeping Safe

There was never a moment when the Barbers would categorize Josh as "mentally ill" or even "temporarily insane." He had always been self-sufficient, highly intelligent, socially adept, and successful in a range of endeavors, including competitive sports, music, and a technical career. He was—no one would dispute it—an intense personality. Over an extended period, perhaps an experienced and sensitive observer would have identified specific areas where Josh's emotional range exceeded some arbitrary norms. Until late in 2009, however, these were pretty similar to the ups and downs of almost any nearly-thirty-year-old single male in the United States. He was functioning quite well in all areas of his life, with more or less dissatisfaction or turbulence at certain times, just like everyone else.

On occasion, beginning in January of 2010, episodes of extreme anguish reduced him to uncontrollable sobbing punctuated by angry outbursts and almost catatonic silences. But even in these periods, a lucid and rational Josh would wake up the following day and sweep aside worries and frowns. If these fluctuations were brought on by something more extreme than heartache and depression, no one mentioned it. The imaginary minute-by-minute observer might have suspected mild bipolar disorder, but the clinicians observing acute symptoms didn't have any reason to turn to that page. And even if they had, was there any more effective treatment or better support system to be offered to Josh and his family?

Josh was very lucid when he argued about his own right to determine his life's course. Maggie recalls a number of such conversations. "Throughout his admissions, he was completely of sane mind, essentially just telling people that he just didn't want to be here anymore and 'How is it OK for you to force me to live when I don't want to?'" He quickly realized, however, that such discussions would not extricate him from the involuntary hospitalizations. He didn't stop talking about it but limited his audience to his family and one or two close friends. "I would go and visit him, and he would talk to me just like it was a matter of fact," said Maggie. "The bottom line was, it was his life, and he was going to do what he wanted with it."

During one stay, he had asked one of the doctors, "Why do you think this [suicide] is not a valid treatment for me?" The doctor replied, "If you were terminally ill, and there was no hope for you, then I agree, that might be the path for you. But that's not you. You have so much to live for, and you've just got to get a little better, so you can get off this obsession, and you'll start to thrive again."

Even if Josh didn't believe this, John, Darla, and Maggie believed it fervently. Each time he went down, they believed it would be the turning point. He would hit bottom and bounce back; the nightmare would be over. They just had to keep him safe long enough.

To keep Josh safe when he was in danger of ending his own life, family members called 911 and invoked a system of response that is based upon a set of policies and assumptions. For example, both police and ambulance response to such a call would be reasonable to expect. Once they are on the scene, police and EMT's are required to conform to standardized procedures. If the family calls 911 and engages these services, they have to abide by the policies. Strong vocal advocacy *may* influence the process, but this is not necessarily the case.

Because of his stated intent to harm himself as reported by his family members, and then because of his failed attempt, Josh was committed to involuntary hospitalization in the psychiatric wards of two different hospitals. When the situation was beyond their abilities and Josh was in grave danger, Maggie or Darla called upon public services paid for by taxes. They felt confident that Josh would (1) be kept safe, (2) be connected with experienced and supportive professionals, and (3) be given treatments/medications that would improve his condition. The experience did not prove to be as beneficial as they had hoped. Josh was kept safe from harming himself, but they were vastly disappointed on the other two hoped-for results. In fact, they might even insist that some of the enforced treatments were actually harmful.

Josh and his family were living through the best that the health care system could offer, and it was very painful and frustrating. Through all of this, they were also experiencing a series of moral dilemmas that, for the most part, had already been decided for them. Many people have written on these issues. Catherine E. Bonn expresses the dilemmas as three questions: "1) Does an individual have the right to commit suicide? 2) Does mental illness exist? and 3) Does the state's interest in suicide prevention allow it to intervene in any way?" Only rarely do Americans contemplate these dilemmas, and never to the extent that would be necessary to bring about deep changes in widespread attitudes. For example, assisted suicide in cases where a person is suffering or terminally ill still remains very limited and controversial in the United States. For someone young and physically healthy, there is *no* case in which choosing to die would be viewed as reasonable. Bonn describes the reasoning thus, "The supposed right to suicide is a derivative right of the right to self-determination, but suicidal people are often irrational and therefore the right to self-determination is meaningless in this context."

Since early in 2010, Josh had been thinking about ending his life as a real option for relief from the guilt, panic, and suffering he was going through. On several occasions when he spoke about it, a friend or family member would invoke emergency response through 911.

After Maggie decided that she could not leave Josh alone when he was feeling so unsteady on the very day of his release from the hospital, she sent messages to Darla and John to let them know what was going on. "I'm not leaving. I'm staying here. He's worried about his safety."

Josh went to bed and fell asleep. Every couple of hours he would come out of his bedroom and pace around and then turn and get right back in bed. Maggie ordered pizza, but he didn't want to eat. If Josh slept all night, it certainly didn't clear his head or relieve his lethargy. He was just exactly the same on Saturday morning, July 3rd. Maggie was exhausted because she hadn't slept much at all, and she was getting more and more anxious.

When she gave up on sleep, Maggie put her nervous energy to work, and she started cleaning and doing laundry. "Hey, Josh! What are we going to do today? Let's go to the mall! Let's take Austin to the park. We can clean your car." She offered him ideas of four or five activities that would get them out of the house. No. He didn't want anything to do with any of her suggestions. He didn't even respond to her. He got up briefly, took a turn through the living room, and collapsed in his bed.

Maggie continued to update John and Darla in between walking by Josh's room to be sure that he was still there. On one of her sweeps down the hallway, she peeked into the room and saw Josh sitting up in bed staring at his laptop. He was crying, his whole body shaking like a small child who can't be comforted. She entered the room and sat down next to him so that she could see the computer screen. Facebook was open on the screen, and Josh was touching a photo of Angela on the screen and sobbing. "I can't believe she's gone." He touched her face on the screen and repeated the same thing, over and over again. "I can't believe that she doesn't love me anymore."

Maggie didn't want to attempt reasoning with him when he was in this tight loop between the face on the screen and his despair. "Shut the computer! You said you were going to do something with me. Let's go! Get in the shower! Enough of this. You're not helping yourself. Stop staring at the computer screen!"

Josh deflected Maggie's instructions and demanded that she call Angela because he wanted to talk to her. He just wanted to tell her what had happened to him. "What do you think is going to happen if I call her, Josh?" It felt brutal to say these things to her brother. "She told you that she didn't want any contact from you. If she wasn't there for you when you were in the hospital after trying to commit suicide, she's not going to be there for you now."

Nothing was reaching him at a level where he could grasp the futility of his strategy. He begged Maggie and told her that she was the only person he had left; nobody else could or would help him.

Finally, he snapped the laptop shut. "I did it. I shut the computer and I'm not looking at her anymore. Now, call her!"

Maggie held out through another sequence or two, and then Josh got angry. He stopped crying and put his energy into shouting at his sister. "Leave! If you're not going to help me, I don't want you here! Leave!"

It was a verbal blow that hit her unexpectedly right in the heart. There was a momentary standoff between the equally strong-willed siblings, and then Maggie burst into tears. She knew that, no matter what, it was better for Josh if she stayed, so she would have to give in. "You're not—it isn't fair, what you're doing to me! I'm trying to help you, and I know that this is only going to upset you more. If you want me to call her, fine. I'll call her. You're torturing both of us!"

Maggie went outside with the phone, and Josh stood at the door watching her. She dialed the number, shaking. Maggie had no gifts at lying; she hoped that Angela would not answer. *"Please, don't pick up! Please, don't pick up!"*

She held the image in her mind of her own number appearing on Angela's caller ID. No answer. If she didn't leave a message, Josh would insist she call again and do so, and they would be back on the seesaw of just a few minutes ago. At the sound of the beep, she forced herself to speak in anticipation of his anger if she didn't. "Angela, it's Maggie. Josh wanted me to call you. Give me a call when you get a chance." When she came back to the door, Josh demanded to know what happened. "I left a message. She didn't answer. I can't do anything else now. I tried. I called her and left a message. I can't make her call me back."

Maggie didn't want Angela to call back, but Josh clung to the thin thread of hope that she would, and that somehow, after all these months of final ending after final ending, this time it would come out differently. He was hoping for the old comfort that, in his memory, her voice always brought him. For the remainder of the day, he was on edge. "Did she call back? Did you hear from her? Did you hear from her?" He would go lie down on his bed, sleep for an hour, and then come out to pace the room and say, "Did you hear from her?"

Josh was desperate for a different outcome with Angela, and Maggie was beginning to feel that there would *never* be a different outcome for her brother—that he was stuck in a vacillation between hopeless anxiety and hopeful illusion. By now, the situation had almost nothing to do with Angela. There are countless blues songs that catalog all the ways relationships end. Josh and Angela once had a vibrant and loving relationship with a glowing future. They both saw a picture of "family" that included each other. That prospect had changed, slowly over time, and then, precipitously, like a derailed train, it had plunged over a cliff. There was absolutely no chance of ever getting back on track. Angela was building a new life, with a career and new relationships. Josh was clinging to the wreck, months later, with pain as fresh and urgent as blood pumping from an artery.

Josh was drained emotionally, but he had been sleeping on and off all day, and he had enough nervous energy to alarm Maggie, just as her energy was flagging from the grueling vigil. She had been in touch with their parents every couple of hours. Maggie remembers, "I wanted somebody else there. I was afraid, and I was starting to get a little loopy myself. I didn't know what to do. It had been twenty-four hours, and we were in the same situation. I was not going to bring him back to the hospital that had just sent him home."

In Jamestown, Darla and John had been on pins and needles all day, waiting for Maggie's next text message. Darla even called Butler Hospital and asked for advice. Their only suggestion was to bring Josh back to the emergency room and begin the whole process of involuntary commitment again. The three of them knew Josh would fight that with his whole being, and by this time, none of them believed that yet another forced inpatient stay was going to fix the problem. It hadn't helped much in the past, and perhaps had made things worse.

Darla had also called Josh's favorite cousin, Stevie, who had told them he would be prepared to come at any time if he could help. Darla hoped that having Stevie come down to be with Josh would help him snap out of this state. Stevie had always been a phenomenal source of strength for Josh. In April, when Josh had not been able to leave the house, Stevie convinced him to drive to New Hampshire for a week. He had a way of getting through to Josh because there was never any bullshit between them. Josh appreciated that. Most of all, Stevie could make Josh laugh.

Late Saturday afternoon, Maggie mentioned to Josh that Stevie was coming, thinking that he would be distracted from his downward spiral and maybe even look forward to the visit. But Josh was furious. He was self-aware enough to reject the idea of anyone besides Maggie seeing him in his current state. "Tell him not to come! If he comes, I'm not going to be here. You asked him to come; now, you tell him to stop. I'm not going to see anybody." Josh picked up all of his medication and put it in his backpack. He was clearly going to act on his words. He was on full alert, out of bed, dressed, sitting opposite Maggie holding his backpack, and poised to leave.

"Josh, Stevie is on his way from New Hampshire; there's nothing I can do; he's almost here." Josh's eyes turned toward some inner reflection, and Maggie could see he was making plans for something. He got up and found a pad of paper and sat down to write.

Maggie continued to present the visit as a positive turn of events, trying to channel Stevie's energy to persuade Josh. "I sent Stevie a text and he said he's coming. He said to tell you, 'Cut the bullshit and suck it up! I'm coming.'" Josh scarcely lifted his head as she spoke. He crumpled a piece of paper and threw it across the room. He started to write again very intensely.

"What are you writing about?" Maggie was keeping her voice as calm as she could so as not to provoke Josh. She was hoping that Stevie would arrive soon and defuse the situation. Josh didn't answer her. He wrote like a man with a ticking time bomb in his head. He had a mission. When Josh finished writing, he had three pages in his hand. He folded them and put them in his backpack. With a defiant glance at Maggie, he got up and went outside but was only gone for a moment.

"Give me your keys!" Maggie's car was blocking his car. "No, you're not taking my car! I don't want you to leave. I'm worried for you; please don't leave. If you want to go for a ride, I'll come with you."

Josh found Maggie's purse and he took her keys. She was prepared to use her entire arsenal of reasoning, empathy, and persuasion, but she would not, could not, attempt physical restraint, even though she sensed he was in imminent danger. Josh scooped up Austin and walked out the door. Maggie watched him speed away in her car with the dog, and she burst into tears. She was frustrated that, with the combined intelligence, education, and experience of three adults, they had no better strategy on the 4th of July weekend than to observe Josh's crisis and potentially destructive actions. The options available through counseling, outpatient-, and inpatient professional encounters and facilities had been futile more often than therapeutic. Medications had not been effective. She allowed herself to feel the full impact of being helpless and alone. She wept.

After the release of simply letting tears flow, Maggie noticed that Josh's backpack was still on the couch. Without regard for his privacy, she opened it and removed the three pages that he had written not long before.

> *Mom & Dad—I've always had the ability to put my complicated thoughts down on paper, although for this one, I feel pretty blank. There's too much time, and too many memories in the past 30 years. With you and I, with Maggie, and all the family & friends that crossed our way. Although I knew it was hurtful, and I did feel guilt, I consciously pushed you two away. Mainly for my own selfishness, but also to maintain my personal freedom. Nothing anyone can say, or prescribe me will fix my shattered heart. Time*

*won't do more than slightly numb the sting of the pain that will
persist till the time I'm gone.*

*I love . . . you Mom, You Austin, You Dad, You Maggie . . . I'm
sorry for the repercussions this will bring all of you. Undoubtedly.
Please try to view it as an end to this cancer that I've had for a
year now, that's only spread with time. Be happy that the boy
or man that remains is now finally free for the first time ever. Be
happy for me in your sadness . . . Take care of Austin!*

There it was, the classic letter saying goodbye to everyone he
loved. Maggie was holding in her hands Josh's suicide note. He
expressed responsibility for his own anguish and loss, love and thanks
to friends and family, and deep sorrow for the pain his actions may
cause to others.

Maggie called Darla, still sobbing, "What do I do? What do I
do? I don't know where he's going. I think I need to call the police
again, but they failed us. I don't want him to go back to the hospital.
What do I do?" Darla and John, though unwelcome at their son's
home, got immediately into their car and drove to Bristol to be with
Maggie.

There was a very large bridge not far from Josh's house, and
Maggie felt sure that Josh was heading there. She called the police and
reported that her brother had taken her car without her permission
and that she had found a suicide note. She gave them her license plate
number and a description of the car.

Josh's house was on Metacom Avenue in Bristol. It is always a
very busy road, especially in the summer. On the 4th of July weekend,
it is jammed. Bristol has one of the largest 4th of July parades in the
country. It claims to be the oldest continuous celebration of its kind,
beginning in 1785. Metacom Avenue was the busiest street during
one of the most populous celebrations, on possibly the most hectic
holiday weekend of the summer.

The police put out a bulletin on the car. Maggie calmed herself down and was trying to call Josh on his cell phone. Her calls were going to his voice mail, and she surmised that he was on the phone with someone else. She alerted the police that they might be able to locate him by the GPS feature of his phone.

John and Darla arrived at the house just moments before the police called Maggie to say that they had found her car. "What about my brother?" "We have him, too. He's in the back of the cruiser. We need you to come get your car right away. We're on Metacom Avenue. We're right near the house."

Maggie stepped outside and looked down the street. She could see her car and the police car pulled off along the side of the busy road. While she was running toward the cars, her phone rang. It was Josh calling from the back of the police car. "How could you do this to me? I can't believe you called the police!" He was furious with her. Completely contradicting the note he had written an hour before, Josh now claimed that he was on his way back to the house and that he only needed to take a ride. He hung up before Maggie could speak.

She could see Josh in the back seat of the police car, but she couldn't even make eye contact with him. The police were pressuring her to get in her car and get it out of there. Austin was still in the car, excited by all the activity and jumping from the front seat to the back seat, barking. Cars were flying by in both directions, all in a big hurry to get somewhere else. Maggie got in her own car and talked Austin down to a slightly quieter frame of mind. She turned the car around without incident, drove to the house, and parked. Once again, the family didn't know where the police would take Josh, or what might happen when he got there. It was just exactly twenty-four hours since he had been discharged from the psychiatric ward at Butler.

There are so many unknowns in the very moment that definitive action is called for, so many things that might influence the decision. Maggie didn't know that, while driving around in her car, Josh had been talking on the phone with his cousin Stevie's wife, Mary, with whom he was also very close. Josh didn't know that Maggie would call the police when he left the house. Darla and John didn't know that Josh would demand to be taken to Newport Hospital this time rather than to Rhode Island Hospital, dreading a repeat of his previous experience. Josh didn't know if the new psychiatrist he was scheduled to see in another four days might have the magic combination of skills and treatments to help him heal. None of them knew whether calling the police this time, or any of the other times, had helped Josh or driven him further into despair. What *was* known—a recent suicide attempt, extreme anxiety, and a definitive written announcement of his intentions—justified emergency measures.

Shortly after Maggie and Austin entered the house, Darla and John walked in, and not long after, Stevie arrived from New Hampshire. Josh still had his phone during the time the police were transporting him to the station and then to Newport Hospital for evaluation. He was texting Stevie periodically throughout the evening, with updates on his location. He didn't know that his parents were at his house with Maggie and Stevie, but he was vocal and very clear about his anger at Maggie for involving the police. Hours passed.

At about 1:00 AM, Stevie received another text message from Josh. "Can you come to Newport and pick me up? If they know I'm going home in your care, they will let me go."

The four of them were shocked that, with all that had happened in the past twenty-four hours and in the past two weeks, Josh still might be released so quickly. The message implied, however, that if Stevie did *not* go to Newport, Josh would not be released. It is difficult, if not impossible, to refuse a direct request for help from a close family member, even when that request leads to consequences that are not welcome or beneficial. Stevie felt compelled to go to his cousin's aid, and Maggie jumped up to go with him. "He's mad at me, but I'm going anyway, because I want to be there."

Maggie was fairly certain that the health care workers would ask to speak with her or Stevie about what had occurred and that they would then decide to keep Josh under observation. She had given the suicide note to the police, and she assumed that this had been passed along to the hospital personnel. She and Stevie sat in the waiting area of the emergency department for several hours. Josh would occasionally send Stevie a text message, just to be sure he was still there. Maggie spoke with the guard on duty. "My brother Josh is here because he is suicidal. I think the doctor will probably want to talk to me before they discharge him."

The guard would say nothing more than, "The doctors will let us know when they are ready to talk to you."

It was still dark outside when Josh came walking unescorted through the double doors from the treatment area. He ignored Maggie entirely and addressed his cousin, "Let's go!"

Two weeks ago, he had hung himself. Twenty-four hours ago, he had been lethargic and sobbing and saying he was worried for his own safety. Ten hours ago, he had written a three-page suicide note and stormed off in his sister's car. Apparently, in the past four or five hours, he had been able to focus all of his energy on the performance of being a mature and rational adult recovering from a discrete episode of regretful self-harm. Possibly, he had even described his parents and sister as extreme in their own anxiety. Whatever he said or did, it worked. He was released to a family member with no further constraints. As relieved as Josh felt to be set free, Maggie and his parents felt equal concern.

Darla and John had left Bristol and returned to Jamestown when Maggie and Stevie left for the hospital. Maggie went home when they returned to the house, and Stevie stayed with Josh for over a week. They went to counseling appointments together, and all seemed to settle into a routine with fairly regular hours of sleep and waking and various purposeful activities filling the days. Josh's cousin Rick came to stay for a few days while Stevie was there.

Everyone, even Josh, could see that he was doing much better when there was another adult in the house with him. He wasn't alone to sink into long periods of thinking about mistakes of the past and lost opportunities for happiness. Stevie, in particular, with a combination of silly jokes and sharp chiding, could always distract him from the lurking sadness and cheer him through another day. Stevie also helped soften Josh's anger against his parents.

Not long after the cousins left, there was another call to the Bristol police by an anonymous caller who said that Josh had been making suicidal comments to her in text messages. The police showed up at his house unannounced for a safety check. In fact, Josh was guiding the rope over a beam when he saw the police pull up and park across the street. He later admitted to his parents, "That was a close one." He managed to hide the rope and convinced the officers that he was stable. He told them that, if they had any doubts, they could call his parents to come over and stay with him. That seemed a reasonable course of action, and John and Darla drove over immediately upon receiving the call. The officers asked them if they would stay there and make sure he was safe. The answer was obvious.

From that point on, the household consisted of Josh and Austin along with Darla and John. It was not easy. Josh didn't want anyone in the house, but he knew the alternative was to be hospitalized again. At times, he was somewhat social, but most of the time, he kept away from his parents in another part of the house. When he would insist that they leave him alone, they replied, "All you have to do is tell us that you are safe."

He couldn't even say those words, let alone feel that much commitment to the future. He would not lie. Darla and John were prepared to stay indefinitely. They handled all of the household tasks, and John either logged into work from Bristol or drove to Newport.

CHAPTER VIII

Becoming the Blues

The blues is an autobiographical chronicle
of personal catastrophe expressed lyrically.
Ralph Ellison

ACCORDING TO ETHAN TODRAS-WHITEHILL IN the *New York Times*, "Costa Rica is an inkblot for projecting travel fantasies . . . [it is] tiny, smaller than West Virginia, but huge in versatility, with coasts on two oceans, coral-lined beaches and active volcanoes, luxury resorts and surf camps, roaring streams and rich biodiversity." Way back in 2009, Maggie and Justin had booked a trip to Costa Rica to attend the wedding of friends. Justin was actually in the wedding, and they would disappoint a lot of people and lose a lot of money if they cancelled the trip. Maggie was reluctant to be so far away from Josh, but with Darla and John staying at his house, she knew he would be safe. She had been right beside him or within thirty minutes of him for months, and it hadn't helped much. By now, she had put so many things on hold to rescue Josh in various emergencies that she had almost lost the pleasures of living her own separate life. Everyone agreed that Maggie and Justin should take the trip to Costa Rica.

Toward the end of July, they left Rhode Island for an open air resort hotel in the middle of the Costa Rican jungle. Cell phones didn't work there, and the only Internet access was a single computer in the hotel lobby. Maggie was looking out on lush tropical vegetation when she opened her email account each day to check on how things were going at home. For the first few days, she was still a bundle of nerves, but gradually, the festivities and gorgeous surroundings penetrated to her core, and she allowed herself to stop worrying and just be a twenty-something on a once-in-a-lifetime holiday with her lover and friends.

Darla replied to her messages of "How are things?" with equally brief messages assuring Maggie that all was going well. "We're fine. Things are the same."

In the back of her mind, Maggie wondered if her mother was putting a positive spin on things so that she would relax and have a good time. But then a bird with bright plumage would flash by, or a strange sluggish lizard would be staring at her, or the bridesmaids would be calling her to join in for a walk on the beach, and she would let the thoughts of crisis drift away.

On the Home Front

One day in early August, John logged onto the server at work from Josh's back deck and was absorbed in the usual press of e-mails, deadlines, and reports. In late morning, he realized he hadn't seen Austin for quite a while. He checked in the house and saw that the dog's collar was in the kitchen. Josh's property was surrounded by an electric wire that would warn Austin with a gentle zap to his collar when he approached the boundaries. Beyond that wire was a busy highway, no place for a diminutive dark shadow of a dog. John panicked; the dog must have slipped out when he opened the door, but without his collar, who knows where he would be by now.

Josh was still sleeping while his father frantically circled the house calling the dog. The thought that went through John's head was that Austin would have escaped the yard and encountered speeding vehicles. He dreaded the sound of screeching tires that he feared would reach his ears at any second.

When John returned to the deck, Josh had just emerged. He was still half-asleep, but picking up on his father's agitation, he asked, "What's the matter with you?"

John hesitated for a beat but knew he had to speak up quickly. "I let Austin out without the collar. I can't find him!" Josh didn't say anything. He just walked around the side of the house, and soon the tall one and the short one came strolling back with neither of them showing the slightest concern. Josh must have known exactly where the dog would be.

John was astonished but even more relieved. He didn't want to think about the impact on his son if that dog had been hit by a car and injured or killed. Josh casually said to his father, "He won't go anywhere. With or without the collar, he won't go out of the yard." The two buddies went back in the house, and John tried to regain his composure and concentrate on work.

Long Hot Summer

One way of describing the hot, humid weeks of July and August, 2010, in the Barber family chronicles is simply as a long, slow-motion blur of constant, low-level crisis and damage control. After the turmoil of the 4th of July weekend hospital discharge and emergency room visit, no one was thinking that another hospitalization would be beneficial. No one was giving up either, but they were in a holding pattern of sorts, hoping that time would begin to heal some wounds, that counseling would produce a breakthrough, or that some combination of drugs would finally relieve Josh of the dark veil over everything good in life. They were not so much patient as exhausted. They had tried everything that was offered. If a new prospect for treatment had opened up, they would have summoned the energy to seek it, but nothing much had changed.

When Maggie and Justin returned from Costa Rica around August 10th, they were refreshed from the change of environment and from being far away from the daily ups and downs with Josh. Maggie had gifts for everyone, and she went to Bristol the day after they returned to visit her parents and Josh. Her hair was a lighter blond from all the sun, and she looked tanned and relaxed. Her gift for Josh was an engraved, hand-made wooden drum. She had been very excited about this gift because of Josh's passion for music. When she saw the drum at a market in Costa Rica, she imagined that he would immediately pick it up and try it out and that they would laugh over how easily he could beat out rhythms with his hands, making them up from thin air or filling their ears with familiar rhythms from earlier days.

Josh was not having that kind of a day. He managed to make an appearance for his sister, but he was unshaven and a bit wrinkled around the edges. His friend Evelyn was also visiting. Evelyn was a young woman he had met during one of his hospital stays. The two of them were very comfortable with one another. They seemed to have a kind of short-hand communication and when they were together, they each seemed better able to cope with the world.

Maggie gave everyone their gifts, and there was a flurry of attention to each item, especially the drum. Everyone wanted to hold it and try it, except Josh. He was not really interested in any of the items or in hearing about the trip. Maggie had tried to prepare herself for this reaction. She quickly changed the subject and felt herself slipping back into the serious and watchful person who gave all of her attention to her brother's issues, carefully reading his facial expressions, words, and actions moment by moment for signs of danger or improvement.

John and Darla had taken the occasion of Maggie's return to plan a barbecue for dinner. John was doing the grilling, and he asked each person whether they wanted chicken or hamburgers. Josh gave this no more attention than he had given the drum. "I don't care; I don't care; I don't care!"

Even after weeks of his extreme and painful disinterest, no one was immune. A small stinging current ran through the rest of the family. John mumbled to himself as he put both a piece of chicken and a burger on the grill for Josh, just in case he might have enough appetite to eat anything at all.

Maggie and Darla were in the kitchen making a salad when they heard a loud noise outside on the deck. Maggie ran out to see what had happened. Josh had kicked out several of the balusters of the deck railing. John, still at the grill, was staring at the gap with a spatula in his hand. Josh had stormed off. Again.

As so many times before, he had been seeking out photographs of his former girlfriend on the Internet. She had removed him from access to her own Facebook pages, but he never got over being curious about her life, especially during his darker melancholy moods, and he kept trying to find any bit of information about what she was doing. On occasion he was successful, but it was a backwards kind of success: it always hurt and it always precipitated a downward spiral. Yet, he kept doing it. Computer scientist Jaron Lanier warns, "If you love a medium that is made of software, there's a danger that you will become entrapped in someone else's recent careless thoughts." He further entreats, "Struggle against that!"

Josh's struggle to resist entrapment in Facebook was not successful. He had come across a new photograph that precipitated the old anxieties. Maggie had been back in Josh's orbit for little more than an hour, and already a new crisis was brewing and she was searching for her brother. Darla and John seemed weary of the drama. John kept his eyes on the grill, turning the meat as it cooked. Darla put her head in her hands for a moment, and then shook off the bad vibes. To no one in particular, she asserted, "I'm just not going there, Josh! Not tonight!"

It was getting dark and Josh hadn't gone far. Maggie found him in just a few minutes. He was standing quite still and alone in the dusky shadows just around the corner of the house. "Josh? Are you all right?"

He lifted his head and looked directly at his sister, but didn't speak. Body language spoke for him. *Leave me alone! Get away from me!* He walked away, and after a couple of beats to recover, Maggie turned and went back inside the house.

They heard the car start up in the garage and moments later, Evelyn, who had been sitting quietly in the kitchen, looked at her phone and read a message. As she was tapping out a response, she said, "He wants to go for a ride. We'll be back later."

Darla, John, and Maggie didn't even protest, and they sat down to eat in silence. John was steaming at the futility of the perpetual disruption of their lives. Darla tried her best to salvage some family connectedness by asking Maggie questions about Costa Rica and the wedding. None of them could really relax and enjoy the summer evening.

After dinner, Maggie tried to get Josh to respond to text messages about when he might return. She had to be up early for work the next morning and would have liked to give him a good-night hug. He didn't respond and didn't return, and finally, she decided to leave.

It was quiet but for the sounds of a few crickets and the hum of traffic as Maggie walked to her car after sharing a group hug with her parents. She felt like she was in a scene from a movie, but she was unsure what kind of movie it was. She knew what the musical score sounded like. It was a single flute, soft and sad, with a melody that didn't build to an end with crashing cymbals but dissipated to a few last notes floating off into the night. It might even be the last scene in the movie, an ending filled with uncertainty as the young woman drives off into the darkness. Before the credits roll up on the screen, the last lines of T.S. Eliot's "The Hollow Men" appear starkly on a black background. "This is the way the world ends/Not with a bang but a whimper."

Her headlights stabbed a path forward through the warm summer night, and Maggie followed. Justin was waiting for her at home, and she couldn't wait to feel his arms around her.

Sweet Escape

Perhaps the most disturbing aspect of Josh's situation was that his distress and behavior didn't fit neatly into any of the categories that are successfully treated with existing methods. His depression was not a textbook case responding to textbook treatments. He always denied symptoms of the mania that would have classified him as bipolar. He was not schizophrenic or delusional, and he was not even slightly mentally ill in any of the ways that indicate a clear treatment protocol with guaranteed results. His family was intelligently marshaling all the resources available, and therefore, he was receiving all of the following: crisis intervention by police, EMT, and emergency room services; involuntary commitment for suicide prevention, psychiatric observation, evaluation, and prescription of various pharmacological treatments; counseling, cognitive behavioral therapy, and assistance/surveillance by family and friends. His attitude toward all of this intervention and treatment was hesitant at best and belligerent and non-compliant at worst.

Those who study the historical and cultural aspects of disease and illness step back from details of techniques and dosages to offer broad concepts about what might be going on when an epidemic of a particular type of illness occurs. Depression, according to some, is one of the defining illnesses of our time, epidemic in its proportions. In his book, *Manufacturing Depression: The Secret History of a Modern Disease,* Gary Greenberg says "Every new climate of opinion about who we are has its distinctive form of lousy weather. Clinical depression—unhappiness rendered as disease—is ours . . . It could be that the depression epidemic is not so much the discovery of a long-unrecognized disease but a reconstitution of a broad swath of human experience as illness." If Greenberg and others are right, the questions being asked about the epidemic of depression must include not only genetic and chemical causes, but cultural ones as well. In *Illness and Culture in the Postmodern Age,* David B. Morris offers the observation that "Depression might be imagined as the reverse of everything our culture admires: it cancels our romance with speed, reducing the sufferer to a near comatose immobility, creating a pleasureless, profitless gloom that drags down anything lighthearted or joyous. It is as if in a single illness the frantic do-it-all, have-it-all lifestyle . . . crashes to a halt."

Josh was living at the intersection of all of these factors and forces—his genetic inheritance, the vicissitudes of neurotransmitter and substance interactions, social pressures and challenges including omnipresent technological devices, voluntary and involuntary therapies, conflicting personal interventions, and more. Some days, he was rendered immobile from the strain, and some days he just managed to put one foot in front of the other to function. When necessary to attain his freedom, he could rebound from a crisis and conduct himself as the bright and engaging talent everyone recognized. This complexity, unfortunately, left him just out of reach of all well-meaning family members, friends, and health professionals.

Josh wrote a poem, possibly in this period after his final hospitalization, that he called "Move On." In the poem he recalls a number of close encounters with death, and he comes to two conclusions: (one) that it had not been his fate to die of any of these accidents, and (two) that death was a *sweet escape* that he once feared, but feared no longer because everyone *moves on.*

Move On

So when did it change?
I had feared it as a child, but now it is gone.
It is escape of sweet fate, 'cause we all move on.

How thrilled must you be with this life
To fear the end of your reign?
It's escape of sweet fate, 'cause we all move on.

The fevers would come, and render me numb
The world sped up as I cowered in fear
Is it, they thought, is it this right here?
No, not my fate, but we all move on.

When I was a boy, I fell from an edge
The ground rose up to meet me instead.
As I staggered around, he found me in a daze
It was not my fate, although we all move on.

Struck by a stone and left alone, crimson painted the street below
I wasn't far off from that place, as I felt the heat stream down my face.
But it was not my fate, even though we all move on.

Passing through the thin ice, day becomes night.
Flash of light, reveals your plight
"Don't pull yourself up, Son. It's worse if you fight!"

Out in the distance, their backs are turned
My screams fall short, is it my fate to be learned?
Then just one last roar, one last before I let go.
Their heads turn and now they know.
So it was not my fate, even though we all move on.

I cannot understand the fear you see
It's just not the same world to me
Perhaps it's wrong to see fit, wherever it may sit
But I ponder this sweet fate, 'cause we all move on.

He mentions a number of childhood traumas in between the refrain of *we all move on.* In some contexts, these words might mean a change of location, change of career, development from one stage of life to another. There is no doubt in the minds of his family that what Josh meant was the transition between life and death.

Respite and Relief

During the month of August, the most therapeutic remedy for Josh was a visit from Melissa Ceprano. She first met Darla and John at Josh's house in early August. "I'm not sure if Josh prepared them for my loudness, energy and enthusiasm. I think I scared them at first."

Sometimes the four of them would just sit around talking, sipping cocktails, and laughing on the deck, but her presence lifted the cloud that seemed to hang over Josh at all other times. Darla and John became very fond of this energetic and generous woman who could make their son smile and converse as if everything in life were just fine. They would have dinner together and play with Austin like old friends do on a summer night. They might end up talking about anything at all, staying away from topics that might bring on Josh's anxiety. Melissa made a point of coming over as often as she could.

"Darla and John noticed that every time I came over, Josh smiled and was very talkative like he wasn't going through hard times in his life. I started to notice it as well so I made even more of an effort to be there for him as much as I could."

Melissa and Josh also made plans to get out of the house. They spent a "Sunday Funday" together on August 8th. "When we were together, he never acted like something was bothering him . . . that he was hurting. He was always so talkative to a point where I couldn't shut him up!" A photo taken that day shows the two friends wearing sunglasses in bright sunshine, smiling broadly with plastic cups of beer in their hands. Behind them a summer crowd is mingling and migrating from one easy pleasure to another.

Darla and John were floating on a high because Josh seemed to be getting better by mid-August. He was working on a new car that he'd bought, and he was even thinking about possibly going back to work. They began to hope that this was the beginning of the long-awaited turnaround for Josh. He seemed to be getting a little better each day.

During the time they had been living with Josh, Darla had decided to start seeing a therapist. She had purposely asked Josh for his permission to see the same person he had been referred to. Josh was skeptical at first, but Darla insisted that her selection was based entirely on proximity to the house. She was hoping that Josh would go along with her, and it did work out that way several times. In the back of her mind, Darla knew that she needed to talk to someone herself, but the main strategy had been to get Josh back into treatment. "I really was going for him, not me, even though I needed it at that point, because I felt that I was drowning. We had been there with Josh for weeks on end."

Josh was calmer than he had been in a long time, but this calm brought with it the matter-of-fact statement that he still had a plan.

"One day, when everyone finally believes I'm doing just fine, I'll take things into my own hands and solve my problems for good."

Darla emailed this assertion to the counselor she and Josh were both seeing, and he replied that she must make clear to Josh the consequences of that action, what it would mean to her. "You need to let him know that that's not OK. Tell him that you won't get over it if he does that. If he tries to trick all of us, and then carry out such a plan, his mother will never be the same."

Shortly after this, at a session with both Josh and Darla, the therapist challenged Josh out of the blue, right in the middle of a conversation about something else. He looked directly at him and he said, "Are you safe, Josh?"

Josh said, "Yes." He didn't hesitate or even blink. "Yes. I'm ready to have my house back. I lived with my parents for twenty-some years of my life. I'm thirty years old now, and I want my independence back." Josh had plenty of experience with the actions that were guaranteed to bring his family and friends knocking on his door. He knew that if he could just control those behaviors, he would be left in peace. He also knew the correct responses to give to the psychologist and the psychiatrist to get their support for his independence.

The therapist looked at him. "I think it's OK for your parents to leave. If you're in trouble, you'll let someone know, right?" Josh solemnly agreed, and it was done. Darla and the therapist both felt that he was ready. His promise to call if he needed help or sensed that things were going downhill again was persuasive. When mother and son walked out of the office, they drove back to the house on Metacom Avenue so that Darla could pack up the clothes and other things she and John had in the house. Josh helped Darla load her car and then gave her a big hug.

Over the next ten days, all was quiet and calm in Bristol and in Jamestown. Nothing much was going on, no frantic phone calls, no disturbing text messages, no incidents of note. Josh spoke briefly or exchanged text messages with one of his parents every other day or so, just short "What are you up to? Not much" calls or texts. He and Maggie touched base through messaging, and these were also just quick, short "Hey, Bud! How ya doin'?" kinds of exchanges. Josh seemed to be keeping busy here and there, with friends and with his car and with Austin.

On Friday, August 27th, Josh ran into Chad Seelig when he was pulling into the parking lot at the Naval Base and Chad was just leaving. They both stopped and they spoke for a few minutes. Chad was surprised to see Josh because he knew that he had been on a leave of absence. "Hey, Josh! What's up? Good to see you!"

"Hi, Chad. Not much; just pulling in to sign papers for my Demo. What's up with you?" Chad knew that the Demo, or annual appraisal, might mean a pay raise for Josh, and he hoped it also meant he was planning to return to work soon. Josh seemed to be doing well, and he asked Chad if he had time to grab a beer. "Gosh, I'd love to, but I have to be at this rehearsal dinner in a couple of minutes. Rain check?"

"Sure, man. We'll do it another time. Call me!" Chad thought that Josh was upbeat; there was no guilt trip laid out for saying he couldn't go for a beer. This always seemed a good sign to a friend who had been through so many shifts in mood.

Josh did his business at the office and then stopped in to see Melissa Ceprano. "Come over after work and see my new car. I could use your help!" Melissa was game. "Sure, I'll stop by and watch you drop a transmission!" She drove to Bristol and kept him company for a couple of hours, helping more with loneliness than with mechanics. It was her special gift, and Josh knew it.

On Sunday afternoon, August 29th, Josh helped Rob Mushen move some furniture. Afterwards, they ordered pizza. For dessert, they sat on the front porch and talked for an hour. The two of them didn't need any excuses to get into deep discussions on the meaning of life. They both felt the trust and affection that allowed them to be completely honest. On this particular day, the topic was very serious. "We talked about dying. We talked about what God would think about someone taking his own life. We also talked about what happens after this life."

Afterwards Josh stopped by his parents' house in Jamestown for a brief in-and-out visit, ostensibly to pick up something or other, but possibly just to touch base with both of them and get a hug from his mother.

Change of Tone

Chad noticed a big shift in the tone of text messages from Josh beginning on Monday and into Tuesday. "His negative texts started coming again. He tried calling me on Tuesday, but I was at work late and never got back to him."

Melissa Ceprano was at work on Tuesday also, and she had not been in touch with Josh all day. She and her husband were expecting friends for dinner. After work, she was on a time crunch. She needed to go directly to the grocery store for a few last-minute items and then get home. She checked her phone after teaching her zumba class, and there was a text from Josh. "Are you coming over after work?" She had to turn him down. "I really want you to come over. Bad day for me."

Melissa was in a bind. She couldn't run to Josh this time. "What's up?"

"My ex with another guy on Facebook. I can't take this!!!!" Melissa knew that, even after all these months, the wound was still fresh and deep for Josh. He was bleeding profusely today. "Get in the car and meet me at the grocery store!"

"No."

"Get out of the house and do something!"

"OK! OK!"

"We'll talk later."

Melissa couldn't shake the feeling that Josh needed someone at that moment, not later. She called Darla to tell her that he was having a really bad day, but Darla already knew. Josh was on his way to Jamestown.

In addition to trying to connect with Chad and Melissa, Josh had also called his psychiatrist's office to try to get a prescription for something to help him through the day. He recognized that he needed some help breaking through this onset of extreme anxiety and hopelessness; he needed more than talk therapy. He left three messages for the psychiatrist, but she never called him back. In this unfortunate perfect storm of unavailability, she was having surgery and was out of the office.

"Mom, are you home?"

"I will be in 5 minutes. Are you coming over?"

"Yes. Is Dad home?"

"No, he's fishing. Is everything OK?"

"No. It'll never be OK!"

"I'll see you at home."

Darla stopped and bought cigarettes and raced home in a panic, just as she had done many times before. She also phoned John who was out in the boat. John immediately replied, "Do you want me to come in?" He was willing to turn around if she thought it was a crisis. They had been through so much worse than this, and Josh had been doing so well recently. "No, he's on his way over. I'll let you know what happens."

Josh drove up in his white Volvo with Austin at around 6:00 PM. Darla could see that he had been crying. He came inside and upstairs to the living room. He was crying. "Josh, what happened?" He told his mother all about the new photo he had seen posted on Facebook. She hugged him, wishing that his pain could flow into her just to give him some relief. He hugged her back like a child who feels he is drowning and only this hug from this person will save him.

Darla tried to comfort him by saying that this was just another episode and that he would get over it just as he had done before. "You've got to let this go. Please stay here for a while until you feel better. She isn't worth all this suffering!"

Josh stiffened immediately, and Darla realized her mistake. Any negative comment about Angela still upset him terribly. "I'm going to go!" He made a gesture dismissing her comment and turned away from his mother. He looked around the room as if to see what he might have forgotten. Austin was going crazy, running around and barking at every little flicker of light or sound.

Darla moved toward the stairway. "I'm going to let the dog out." Josh followed her down to ground level. "I'm about to leave anyway." He scooped up the dog.

"Josh, don't go. Come in and take a Xanax or something. Don't leave like this when you are so upset."

"No, I'm leaving." It was just four or five steps to his car, and he was gone.

Darla watched him drive away. A small part of her mind was puzzling over why he was driving his old car when he had that beautiful new Nissan 300ZX he had been working on. On a sultry August day like this, she would have thought he would be driving his pride and joy with the roof down. She went back inside and called John to let him know what had happened. He offered again to come home, but both of them thought Josh was doing well enough to deal with this setback. It was a horrible day to be sure, but he had gotten over so many horrible days just like this one. Since mid-August, he had seemed to be getting back on his feet.

Darla called Maggie and told her about the day's confusing incident. This was such a familiar conversation. Darla wanted to know, "Have you talked to him today? How did he sound?" And Maggie wanted to know, "Should I call him now? Should I text him?"

There was no right answer, they had discovered over months of practice, but they still asked each other the same questions almost daily. On the one hand, they were worried for his safety, but they didn't want to reinforce his downward spirals with their own anxiety. On the other hand, he was a thirty-year-old man, and he was telling them most of the time that he wanted to be left alone.

Darla constantly coached herself to think through what she was in control of and what she wasn't. She knew she had to stop trying to control Josh. That was not in her power.

Maggie had sent many text messages to her brother over the past months that received no answer. She had even sent a few with threats. "If you don't get in touch with me within the hour, I'll have to call the police or come over there." His response was predictable: "Leave me alone."

An hour or so after he left, Darla sent a text message to ask if he was home. She didn't hear from him, so she sent a text to Melissa and learned that she had just heard from him. Darla was reassured that at least he was in contact with Melissa.

Melissa's evening went by in a flash, but even before her guests left, she thought about Josh and sent him another text message.

"Hey, what's up?" No response. She let an hour go by and then she sent another message. No response. She dialed his number, but he didn't pick up. She was getting anxious now about her friend. Josh always responded to her; she was his best pal, his guaranteed smile. This silence was most unusual. Around 10:00 PM, Melissa decided that she must let Darla and John know that she couldn't get Josh to reply to her.

Darla also got no reply to her message and call. John made a call to Josh and demanded, "Answer the phone right now! Josh, answer the phone!" Still, no answer. Darla told Melissa that if they didn't hear from Josh by eleven, they were going to drive to Bristol to check on him. They would keep her in the loop.

Just before eleven, John called his friend Ted Luther who lived just a block or two from Josh. Ted had been involved at least once before, helping John to restrain Josh when he was determined to run off. John asked Ted to go over to Josh's house right away and let them know if he could get Josh to answer the door.

Ted went over at a few minutes after eleven and knocked on the door. He heard the dog bark, and he thought he heard Josh trying to quiet the dog down. Josh didn't come to the door, and Ted didn't want to intrude. He reported what he had heard to John.

Darla said, "John, we have to go. We have to go to Bristol."

John and Darla drove to Bristol that night, as they had so many times before, with mixed emotions. They were concerned, of course, but not in a panic this time. They didn't know that Josh had been trying to get in touch with his psychiatrist or that he had tried and failed to connect with Chad and several other friends. The only people they had communicated with were Melissa and Maggie. Maggie had not been in touch with her brother that day at all.

Josh's psychiatrist had told John on the phone not long before, "Don't worry. I've been doing this a long time. Nothing's going to happen to him." The therapist she recommended also had assured them, just ten days before, that Josh seemed to be doing well enough for them to leave him alone. Josh, himself, had promised them, "I know what I'm doing here." At the time, they just barely registered that this was an ambiguous kind of assurance that could go either way.

They arrived at Josh's house a little after eleven-thirty. John knocked on the door, and there was no answer. This was not a novel situation for them. There had been many times when Josh didn't open the door for them. There had even been one time, months before, when John had broken the lock to get in. Darla suggested that John use his key to unlock the door. "Why don't you just open the door with your key?"

"Because he doesn't want us here. I want *him* to open the door." John was trying to stay focused on a process that respected Josh's adulthood and privacy. In his mind, he was preparing what he would say to his son when he opened the door. Something like, "Sorry to barge in again! You weren't answering your phone, and everyone was worried about you."

Finally, John pulled out his key. "I had a key, and after a minute or two, I used it. It was dark. As the door swung open, I saw him hanging there."

John moved swiftly to grab Josh by the legs and lift him up. He shouted to Darla to get a knife. Darla couldn't see anything, so she was saying, "Why? Why do you need a knife?" as she groped her way through the living room. She couldn't seem to locate a switch to turn on the lights, but she made her way to the kitchen anyway. Step by step, her general sense of alarm from the tone of John's voice converged in a very specific dread that the horrific and unthinkable was happening right now. It couldn't be happening, but it *was* happening.

She remembered the drawer in the kitchen that held the big knives and she opened it, grabbed a knife, and brought it to John. He held Josh up with one arm and cut through the rope with the other. "I thought he was still alive, because every time I lifted him up, I could hear a whoosh of air. I thought he was breathing, but he wasn't."

Darla had called 911 as soon as she handed the knife to John. Until the EMTs arrived, John gave his utmost effort to resuscitate Josh. When they entered with their equipment, he stepped aside, but they didn't move forward. John screamed at them. "Aren't you even going to try!?" Two of them stepped forward and, using a handheld device to force air into the lungs, made a good effort. They knew it was futile but were willing to give Darla and John a few moments more to come to this realization: Josh was gone.

Darla started to weep, covering her face and saying "No! No!" over and over.

John was still flushed with adrenaline, and he was furious. His anger was directed every which way, looking for some satisfying target to blame. He was angry at Josh for not giving them more time, angry at all the medical and mental health providers for not having better tools and skills to help his son, and angry at all the decisions— the enormous decisions and the most miniscule decisions—that had led to this moment. His rage soon subsided, however, and he was filled with grief, regret, and deepest sorrow. There was no escape from this moment for either Darla or John. Before the emergency workers lifted their son out of their lives, Darla knelt down and held him in her arms for one last time. It was traumatically direct and immediate, gruesomely shocking, and at the same time, quite unbelievable. They were filled with the horror, through every pore, through every nerve ending, through every sense of their minds and bodies that wanted to reject it all, to turn back the clock just a few minutes to before they knew this hell.

Shock-waves

Maggie and Justin were sound asleep when her cell phone rang at 3:30 AM on Wednesday, September 1, 2010. The phone was plugged in right beside the bed. Maggie had spoken to her mother at about 10:00 PM on Tuesday night, just before settling down. She knew Josh had visited Darla in the afternoon and that Melissa had heard from him after that. It was a worry, but nothing compared to so many other times. Maggie went to bed and prayed as she had been doing every night for the past year. "I'm not even religious. But every night when I went to bed, I would always ask whatever God there was to please watch over my brother and keep him safe. Keep him safe and help him find happiness. I said the same things every single night when I went to bed."

Maggie answered the phone and heard her father's voice. "Mag, we're outside. Can you let us in?" She knew what had happened the instant she heard her father's voice. She jumped out of bed and ran straight to the door. Her grief-stricken parents were standing there like frozen statues.

"He's gone."

Maggie screamed, "NO!" and threw her arms around both of them. She was not going to believe it. If she rejected the information, then maybe it *wasn't* true, or could be reversed, or they could go back in time. "No! This can't be! This can't be!"

The three of them clutched one another in the doorway, neither in nor out, refusing to admit the moment that they had dreaded for so long. After a minute, Maggie pulled them inside to the living room and Justin, hearing Maggie's shouting, came out of the bedroom. Maggie made herself say the words she could not believe, and Justin began to cry. The four of them were tortured with the assault of reality, futile in their efforts to push it away, and stinging with wave after wave of pain. Darla and John began to tell them a little of what had happened over the past hours. Maggie's impulse was to protect Justin, knowing that he had to get up and go to work in a few hours. She pulled her parents toward the door and said, "We'll leave. Justin, you go back to sleep."

Austin was waiting for them in the truck. Maggie got in with her parents and the dog, and they drove to Jamestown. The house seemed quieter, darker, and emptier than ever before. They felt empty, too. There was no longer any crisis or purpose for their immediate effort—no battles to fight, no adrenaline surge to get them through. This was the ultimate catastrophe and the final defeat. The three of them sat or lay on the couches in the living room, looking at one another, without hope and without a plan.

Maggie fell asleep for an hour or two and when she woke up, she immediately remembered why she was at her parents' house. She began to cry. "I don't want to wake up like this every day, realizing that this is another day without Josh!"

In a way, Josh was still vividly with them in those first hours and days as they made phone calls to family and friends, planned a funeral service, and went through the motions required of them. John could not stop thinking about how this particular time, out of dozens of times standing outside Josh's door in the middle of the night, he had had no inkling of what he might find. "He didn't answer the door; he didn't answer the door. And I'm telling you, it was the last thing on my mind."

John played over and over in his mind all of the ways Josh had behaved that led them all to believe he was coping better and better with life's disappointments. He had bought a new nose and a new back bumper for the Nissan 300ZX, and he was rewiring the whole thing. He sent them photos of his progress. If he had a master plan of deliberately deceiving them about his recovery, it had been successful. They had read the signs of his stability, and so had his psychiatrist and his counselor. They had *all* backed down from crisis mode and were enjoying those few weeks in August, thinking Josh was almost back to his pre-break-up confidence and vitality.

Just when their vigilance was down, a trigger that he had been coached for and prepared for caught him off guard and broke through his defense strategies at a moment when he tried but couldn't activate his safety back-up plans. Facebook provides a temptation and a template that is easy to use and hard to resist. Josh wasn't quite strong enough in his recovery to stay away entirely, and he actually sought out the very arrow that was poisonous only to him. He reached across the Internet and opened his most vulnerable heart to danger. It was a beautiful summer day, struck into tragedy by a most unfortunate "perfect storm" of too-available social media and not-available-enough safety net.

Maggie couldn't stop herself from reflecting on the many times she and Josh had talked about this escape route. She tried every means of persuasion against suicide, including the brutal reality of partial success, of his being alive and permanently incapacitated. "You have no idea what you could end up like," she said to her brother. His response to this was, "I wouldn't mess it up! Even if I did, there's no way anyone else is going to choose what measures are taken to save my life!" She knew that Josh had spoken to a lawyer about this. On the same day that he wrote the list of all of his possessions, and where he wanted them to go, he also signed a living will, affirming that he didn't want any extreme measures taken to save his life. Knowing all this, she put her whole heart into every hug with her brother over those months, just in case this was the last hug she would ever have.

Above all, Maggie knew that Josh would not ever have wanted to hurt his parents by deliberately arranging things so that they would be the ones to find him. There had to be another explanation. As they went over and over the events of the afternoon and evening, she realized that he must have thought the police would reach the house first. There were messages on his phone from his parents saying they were calling the police if he didn't answer.

Even in her dazed state, Darla knew that their love and support had made a difference. "We kept him here a lot longer than he wanted." She had seen the grocery list on his kitchen counter and realized that he didn't get up that morning thinking that it was his last day. She kept reliving the hugs from her son just the day before, when he had arrived at the house crying. It was such a short visit, but they had hugged and hugged. "I didn't realize that he was coming to say goodbye."

Melissa Ceprano woke up on the morning of September 1, 2010 and looked at her messages. She saw that John Barber had sent her a text at around 3:00 AM. "Call me when you get this," was all it said.

"I got up and helped my husband off to work. I took a shower, got dressed, ate breakfast, and sat on my couch with a box of tissues. I called John around 9:00 AM, and he told me what I already knew—Josh was gone."

There were no easy phone calls for the Barbers that day. Every call was excruciating at both ends of the line. There were sobs and tears, a few comments of disbelief, even fewer questions, and many, many expressions of concern. By the afternoon, well-meaning friends and family had begun to arrive. There was nothing to do and not much to say; they just sat together in the living room. Occasionally, someone would begin a sentence or make a statement about Josh.

"I'll never forget how he helped us that time."

"He was so amazing that time he sang and we were all there."

"No one could ever make me laugh like Josh did."

The weather was oppressive with late summer heat and humidity. There is no air conditioning in the Barber house and with people sitting on every available chair and sofa and some out on the deck and even on the floor, the place was thick with sorrow. The TV was on almost constantly to cover the silence, but silence was mostly what everyone heard. There was no escape from the sticky heat, or the uncomfortable stillness, or from thoughts of a young, vital life ended too soon.

The doorbell rang with deliveries of food and flowers. Neighbors brought helpful supplies and wouldn't leave until the kitchen was cleaned and ready for the next day. The palpable support of everyone who showed up to mourn with them kept Maggie, John, and Darla going through the necessary motions of making arrangements for a funeral. Every gift was deeply appreciated even as it was a painful reminder of the reason for the outpouring of generosity. Maggie summed it up for the whole family. "Nothing was good during those days."

Maggie and Darla came across Josh's journal in his room in Jamestown when they were looking for photos for the funeral home. They had seen it before, but now it had more significance to them. "We all took turns reading it within the first week, and we shared parts of it at his funeral. Some pages were displayed on a large board at the funeral home, and Maggie read the letter Josh wrote *to everyone in my life past and present* during the services.

To Everyone in my life past and present.

If anything should happen to me for any reason, I want to have whatever I feel but hesitate saying written down. I love you. I love you all. Those that are my friends and family; in between; and enemies. My parents have been nothing but perfect to me my whole life, and my sister the same. I wish I said that more often. Shit! I wish I said it every once in a while. My anger and unhappiness really seem unwarranted when you look at my sheltered life, so I apologize for any pain or misery I've caused. I myself don't understand it.

Please know that I'm ashamed for my laziness, and lack of ambition. I'm sorry if I ever disappointed anyone. But I do love you all, I hope in some way, you were able to see that underneath my permanent scowl. Thank you for all the love you sent my way. My grandparents and extended family. My best friends, you know who you are. I hope you're able to keep fond memories of me when I'm gone.

Thank you
Love
JOSH

The first week was an ordeal because there were always people around, and there were rituals that everyone expected and that must be arranged. The rituals of obituary, undertaker, viewing, eulogy, and funeral feel excruciating while they are happening, but they provide a semblance of structure and momentum for the most grievous and chaotic pain. The family moved through all as if through neck-high water, pushing a ton of weight with every step and always in danger of drowning.

Despite all the lovingly prepared food delivered by friends, Darla had no appetite and Maggie felt nauseous at the thought of eating. When everyone was there, all they wanted was to be alone, and when everyone left, they felt devastated by the emptiness.

The second week was a struggle for a different set of reasons. People go back to their lives, which do go on much as before, except for those closest to the person who is gone. Darla, John, and Maggie were numbed by the shock of confronting a death that had been threatened many times but that they never really absorbed. When everyone else went home, the three of them were left alone in the house as a swell of feelings and thoughts slowly returned. It was impossible not to think of what they might have done differently, of all the actions and reactions that might have changed this outcome. The blunt impact of the event seemed to reverberate into the past by altering the meaning of everything that had gone before. Decisions that had seemed crystal clear at the time were now on shaky ground. They were nearly sleepless and suffering under the weight of unanswerable questions.

Austin was in the house with them, and his energy and demands forced them to move around, prepare food, take a walk outside. The dog had become so much a part of Josh that having him around was painful in part, but in other ways it was comforting, as if Josh was almost there, too. Austin had brought so much happiness to Josh's life, and that would always be appreciated. Darla had loved the little pug at first sight. Josh knew how attached she was to Austin, and he had even suggested that she get her own puppy. Darla was Austin's "grandmother," and she wouldn't transfer her affection to any other dog. Austin had stayed with them every time Josh was in the hospital, and she had a wisp of a feeling that someday Austin might be living with them on a more permanent basis. It was one of those things that a family member may know subconsciously but doesn't really want to know.

There were truly many other things that they would never know: did Josh adhere to his medication schedule exactly as prescribed? How often did he see a therapist, and what had been the value of their discussions? What was the full power of his anxiety and panic? They would never know these things, but now, Josh's parents and sister had a new series of even more urgent unknowns: how would they go on without him?

CHAPTER IX

We All Move On

If there is no other comfort in a suicide not avoided,
at least there is this persistent thought, that it was an act
of misplaced courage and unfortunate strength rather than
an act of utter weakness or of cowardice.
Andrew Solomon

Tragedy while vast is bearable.
Lucille Clifton

AT FIRST, IT SEEMS THAT the staggering burden of grief will crush you into the ground. Traumatic scenes play over and over again in your head, and the physical ache and exhaustion make you feel as though you've been in a car wreck. Each day feels endless and empty; nothing feels worth doing, and sleep brings not relief but a dreaded and restless wasteland to be endured. What happens next?

Maggie stayed at her parents' house for almost a month. Some nights, she would sleep in her old bedroom on the first floor, and some nights she would sleep on the couch. She couldn't get comfortable anywhere, and she didn't sleep much at all. None of them did. Nighttime was the worst time of all. Maggie was restless and fretful. "I hated even the thought of putting my head down on a pillow with nothing to think about but Josh and all the bad visions that would crowd into my mind."

One night John said, "Why don't you just come up and sleep with us." Maggie couldn't picture it.

"Dad, what do you mean, sleep with us?"

"You sleep in the bed with your mother. I'll sleep on the floor." She couldn't accept this solution, but being close to them was so appealing.

"No, I'm not sleeping in the bed, but I'll sleep on the floor."

Maggie brought cushions and blankets upstairs, and like a small child, she slept on the floor of her parents' bedroom. Austin slept there with her. In the mornings, they were comforted to wake up all together in the same room. Being together was the only thing that made those days bearable. Austin represented what was left of Josh, and they kept him close. The little pug seemed to know his role, and he was attentive and sensitive to each of them.

For Maggie the first three months were a complete blur. "I only remember that Mom, Dad, and I were together all day, every day because that was the only way we could survive. A few times in the initial days, when the gut-wrenching reality really hit me deep down, I would run to the bathroom to vomit. I remember dreading the night time and not being able to sleep. The darkness and silence always led to anxiety and deep sadness. When I lay down to close my eyes at night, I would see visions of the night he died. Over and over, I would relive the moment Mom and Dad knocked on my door, and the minutes, hours, and days following that moment."

Maggie decided to take advantage of some help in getting through this time. "I finally resigned myself to taking anxiety medication so I could fall asleep at night. Still, most nights I would wake up around 3:00 or 4:00 AM. I was out of work for almost a month. The return to work, even with reduced hours, was initially torturous. I would cry the whole way to work and then had to compose myself before entering the building. It felt like I was holding my breath the entire time I was at work, just to get through the day. As soon as I got to the car, I would break down and cry again."

Day by day, she was straining to accept the reality of life without Josh. "I couldn't wait to get back home to be safe with Mom and Dad. They were the only people who understood the torture I felt. I was suddenly an outsider within my work community of people I had previously felt comfortable with. No one understood how sick with sadness I felt. I knew I had to continue going to work every day, however; otherwise I would never get back into the routine. In the long run, working was good for me because it gave me something else to think about and kept me busy."

John recalls the first three months as an extended period of shock. "There were waves of totally devastating emotional crashes, but it was sort of not real—the reality was simply not imaginable, so you don't let it become fact in your brain. You don't believe it. I remember that there were moments where my mind would drift into a daydream for a bit and all of a sudden, wham! I'd remember the reality and it would just suck the life out of me."

Like Maggie, John found it very hard to go out in public and engage with other people. Even though he appreciated the distractions of seeing friends and family, all of those early encounters were very difficult and emotional.

Not long after Josh's funeral, John understood fully how supportive his superiors at work could be. He received an unsolicited offer from upper management that allowed him to telework up to four days a week. He took advantage of the offer and used leave for the fifth day for several weeks until he was ready to gradually begin working on site. His team had been functioning well when John worked from Bristol during the period he and Darla lived with Josh, and this continued. It was many months before John felt ready to resume working full time at the Newport facility.

Darla, unlike John and Maggie, did not return to an office. She remained at home, and she continued to feel the loss incessantly. "I had read earlier parts of Josh's journal a long time ago, but after he died and I came across the journal again, his pain became clearer. We were all still feeling despair, disbelief, sadness, numbness, and guilt. It was a roller coaster ride. When the funeral was over and everyone left, Maggie, John and I were attached like glue. Nobody could ever know our pain. We made all of our decisions together, and we were extremely mindful of each other's feelings. We each had our separate way of loving Josh and of mourning, yet we were very much the same."

As the depth of her son's pain became clearer, Darla—who had always felt empathy for any creature in pain—was in agony. "Now that I realized the excruciating pain that he had been enduring for the past year, I felt my heart had been ripped out of my chest. I knew why he didn't want to live any longer. I felt it to the core. That fact made me feel tremendous guilt that I had tried so hard to keep him here on earth with us. I so wish I had been able to say, 'I understand your pain,' but at the time I *didn't* understand. He suffered here much longer than he wanted to because we believed with all our hearts that he could recover."

All three of the Barbers felt that their source of strength in the early weeks came from one another. Darla said it over and over, "Maggie and John have been my source of strength and my reason for living. Without them I don't know where I'd be."

Gradually, other significant events began to divert the family's attention for short periods. On November 30th, Justin and Maggie signed the final documents on the purchase of their house in North Kingstown. New energy entered the universe, and seeds of the future began to sprout. With impeccable timing, Justin proposed to Maggie the night after the closing on their first home. The very act of congratulating the young couple with words of joy began to thaw hearts frozen for months in deepest grief.

No one forgot about Josh, but there were sometimes moments when the pain could be overcome through positive action. Maggie and Justin moved a few key pieces of Josh's furniture into their house in the beginning of December, 2010. The black leather sofa and the big coffee table that Josh had selected would now live with them. It was finally bearable to have these intimate reminders nearby.

There were many setbacks in the healing process. At about six months after Josh's death, reality set in with a vengeance. John felt that finally, "your brain accepts the fact—you really believe it—and it's even worse than earlier. It brings on the most devastating sorrow, deeper and more constant than before."

March will always be a difficult month for the Barber family, with so many intense memories, both joyful and painful. March of 2011 found Josh's parents and sister functioning at a survival level, taking just one day at a time. As they approached all the family birthdays in March, they could not imagine how they could celebrate these occasions, or even how to live through the days without Josh's presence. It didn't seem possible that they could feel his absence any more sharply, but in March, they learned that new spikes of pain were indeed possible. Maggie recalls their collective wish to "just fast forward through all of it: Dad's and Uncle Charlie's birthdays on the 3rd, mine on the 7th, and then Josh's and Uncle Rob's on the 21st. It was a time that we had always spent together, celebrating with our whole family." Living through all the birthdays of March, 2011, was one of those "firsts" of the torturous twelve months after losing a loved one. The following March might not be any easier, but it would be difficult in a different way.

Josh's house in Bristol was the locus of so much pain that they avoided going there, both physically and psychically. The short visits had very specific purposes: to pick up the sofa and coffee table, to retrieve guitars and other precious memorabilia, and to salvage Josh's paintings. Several of them were framed and mounted, and these were relatively easy to move. The large murals painted directly on the walls were no less treasured but were infinitely more challenging to disconnect and remove to safe storage. John called this project a rescue: "Friends and relatives came to help us rescue the paintings. A good friend who is a builder, and most of Darla's siblings and their spouses, all came with trucks and equipment. We cut the walls out, including the studs, and crated the huge slabs to protect them. Then, we rebuilt the walls so you couldn't tell there were ever any paintings there. The black and white picture which seems to depict Josh in his last seconds was difficult to look at, but I couldn't just leave it. We rescued them all."

Darla's memory is focused on how it felt. "I'm not sure of the date. I only remember the raw emotions and tears when John, his friend John Dourado, and my brothers-in-law delivered the huge pieces of sheetrock, carefully wrapped to protect Josh's art. My sisters were all here with me as we watched them take the last piece off the truck. It was such an emotional Sunday that all of my family decided to stay in Jamestown another night with us. I have the best, most supportive family in the world, and having them near us for this was the only way we got through it."

Minus the paintings, furniture, guitars, and other cherished items, the house in Bristol was a desolate and empty shell, a scene of tragedy. The family had nothing left to care about there, and they let go of any attachment to the place. Their hearts would always be drawn to any signs and locations of Josh's vitality, but there was nothing left of him in that house. They paid the mortgage for many months and offered the house for sale. About a year after his death, they stopped paying and the house went into foreclosure. The bank badgered the family with calls and with letters that were absurdly addressed to "Joshua Barber deceased . . . Not to be opened by anyone other than the addressee."

As the months went by, John, Maggie, and Darla slipped back into ordinary routines, but Josh was never far from their thoughts. When they were together, he was always there, in the conversation, in their minds, in Austin's compact energy. On occasion, they felt even closer to a presence that seeped into life in surprising ways. It might be a song on the radio, or a certain smell that would bring Josh to mind along with the feeling that he was just beyond perception in the room. The persistent stare of a pigeon perched outside the window felt like a message, and they would often dream of Josh in that way that causes the sleeper to question which state is reality or the dream when they wake up. Upon the urging of others, they attended a session with a medium. Darla's love and strong desire to believe in the possibility of spirit contact brought the medium to her side with comforting words in the form of a message from Josh. They received these experiences as consoling gifts to ease the burden of grief, no more and no less.

John's friends made a particular point of encouraging him to be active and to get out of the house. One of them made it his business to get John back into hunting. John recognized the little strategies and went along with them. "When I didn't cooperate at first, my friend called upon me to *help* him transport a deer out of the woods and tend to the handling of the meat. He also had me *help* him place some tree stands—one of which was designated for me. He went to the extent of obtaining exclusive permission from a land owner for me to hunt on his property."

The evidence that his friend was successful is that John took two deer with a crossbow in one season. This man also made sure that John had first refusal for many fishing trips on his boat and even made a significant sacrifice, according to John: "He even accompanied me in my boat on occasion, even though I'm sure he'd rather have taken his own." This is just one example of how many of their devoted friends kept gently nudging the Barbers toward resuming activities.

By the summer of 2011, almost a year later, the whole Barber family was finding that they could shape their grief into specific actions. They were formulating the mission of a non-profit organization that would try to plug the gap exactly in the place where they felt Josh had lost his battle—the danger zone between 24/7 inpatient care and independent outpatient life. They started to tell stories about Josh in preparation for a book that would be part of fundraising for their non-profit. Maggie and Justin were planning a wedding, and this momentum tugged the whole family along.

Memories of Josh on the wedding day of Friday, September 23, 2011, were intensely personal. Maggie wanted it this way. "There was intentionally no large group remembrance, so as not to upset people. I remembered Josh in my own personal way; my "something blue" was a blue guitar pick of Josh's. I wore it around my ankle on a silver chain, and the wedding photographer took pictures of Mom putting it on me. I think Mom and Dad and everyone else were thinking of Josh in their own way, and that was just right!"

By October of 2011, WE ALL MOVE ON was registered with the State of Rhode Island as a non-profit organization, and it was ready to accept funds. Maggie designed the Web site, and the vision of the organization went public: "WAMO's vision is for a safety net of flexible, 24/7 services and resources available for individuals struggling with depression and their families or care-givers."

A benefit concert was held on October 30, 2011, at The Narragansett Café in Jamestown, the site of many performances by Smokestack Lightnin' and J.B. and The Stack. A second similar benefit was held on October 14, 2012. The intention is to continue that tradition indefinitely. One of Josh's guitars is witness to these commemorative events from a glass display case high on the wall. Photos of Josh and Smokestack Lightnin' in performance at the "Ganny" had already been installed before the first benefit.

The Jamestown Press and *The Providence Journal* both covered the 2011 concert. In announcing the concert ten days before it took place, the Jamestown paper noted that Smokestack Lightnin' was "a fixture at the Narragansett Café which became Josh's favorite place to play." The article also mentioned the two awards from the Providence Phoenix for "Best Blues Act" in 2004 and 2008. The *Journal's* extensive coverage of the event published on November 13, 2011—"Out of Despair, Hope for Others" by Rick Massimo— included interviews with the family as well as with other musicians and Butler Hospital's associate vice-president, James W. Alves. The Barber family met with Alves several months after the suicide, and he joined them in envisioning "a pilot program to bridge the gap" between inpatient care and life outside the hospital. The article points out that "Recent federal studies reveal that Rhode Island has the highest rate of mental illness and the highest percentage of adults who have planned or attempted suicide. While those same studies show that the completed rate among Rhode Islanders is fairly low, finding the kind of care that can save a life is a difficult process."

The *Journal* article comments on the numbers of musicians who showed up to play in memory of Josh: "singer Nino Paldan, the father-and-son rhythm section of Chad and Dick Souza and pianist Mark Taber, joined by the terrific guitarist Tom Ferraro. At the end, it turned into a jam session with Rhode Island blues stalwarts including guitarist Neal Vitullo, singer Dave Howard, and Roomful of Blues pianist Travis Colby among those sitting in." Vitullo said, "[Josh] really loved music. Every time I saw him, he was happy and very excited about playing." Mark Taber caught the spirit of the event when he said, "[Josh] is probably walking around here somewhere." In addition to Josh's photo on the walls and on the tee-shirts, he was vivid in everyone's minds as they listened to the music he loved. Both articles foreground the creation of WAMO as an effort to help others striving to overcome depression.

The positive vibrations from the event were magnified for the inner circle with breaking news of another kind. Maggie was pregnant. "I found out I was pregnant just before the first benefit event at the end of October 2011. I couldn't believe it at first. I think I took three home pregnancy tests! Justin and I were so happy, and I couldn't wait to tell Mom and Dad. I called Mom and said something like, 'I'm just wondering . . . can you have a false positive home pregnancy test?' She was beyond excited and wanted to tell everyone right away. I made her keep it a secret from everyone except Dad until I was past twelve weeks."

"Dad was out of town when I found out, and I asked him to meet me on his way home from the airport. I used an excuse about planning for the benefit. When I saw him, I hugged him and told him that if all went well, he was going to be a Poppy in July. We both cried."

"Without a doubt, this was the happiness we all needed after just passing the one year anniversary of losing Josh. The thought of a baby gave us hope that there would be joy in our lives again."

When Maggie was just a few weeks along in the pregnancy, she and Darla and John visited the medium again. This time, the medium spoke of a new life that was coming into the family and told them that Josh was spending lots of time with that new soul. They didn't need to be told that Josh would have been very happy for all of them.

As the second anniversary of Josh's death approached, so did the birth of Ava. She seemed to come just in time to be a most appreciated birthday gift for Darla! "On July 13th, the day after my birthday, Maggie and Justin blessed us with a beautiful baby girl named Ava Snow Barber-Leclerc. Snow is my maiden name and Maggie's middle name. I now have a reason to get out of bed in the mornings. She has brought me so much joy and feelings of purpose and self-worth, as I have the privilege of caring for her when Maggie goes to work."

After the second benefit to raise money for WAMO in October, 2012, Maggie talked about the event: "We had new tee-shirts made with Josh's signature 'JAB' on the front, exactly as he signed them on his artwork. More than anything, it was good to have everyone together, remembering Josh and enjoying the music he loved so much." Maggie spoke to the crowd to keep them up to date on progress with the book and with fundraising.

In the ordinary days that move along without big events, the Barber family moves forward step by step, just like countless other families. Every new gurgle or gesture from Ava sends a news flash throughout the family. Things look calm and peaceful, but there is a heightened sense of what's important in this family.

Darla reflects on life today, more than two years after she lost her only son.

> My days are still pretty much the same. I am functioning better. Sometimes I worry a lot and don't sleep much, which makes it difficult to want to get out of bed in the morning. My life is still sad, and I long for the life I was

so blessed with before. That won't happen. Our lives are forever changed.

I worry about the future, but I am grateful for all I have: my great husband, my phenomenal daughter, my wonderful son-in-law, and my incredibly sweet Ava.

My extended family and friends have been there for us all along the way. They are always at the other end of the phone or driving here, and some don't even hesitate to jump on a plane to be with us at a moment's notice. Even our community has reached out to us and has helped us with our non-profit organization. We *can* make a difference together in what happens to people with depression. We *will* make a difference. We *ARE* making a difference.

Maggie also finds that, however it appears on the surface, life now "is completely different. It will *never* be the same. I've had people ask me about this and I always tell them that I don't even really remember what life was like before this whole traumatic experience. Now, every day counts, family is the most important thing in my life, and the little things just don't matter anymore."

There is a type of balance that the Barbers seek constantly. Their daily lives involve meaningful work and carefree play, sunny days on the water and darker days on icy roads. They get together with friends, and they take pleasure in family time, boating and fishing, and even in the simple things like coming home to a kitchen that smells like cinnamon and spice. Most especially, they take great joy in Ava's every smile, chuckle, and wiggle. She is the sun, the moon, and the stars. All of this provides equilibrium against memories of devastating trauma, feelings of helplessness, and the abiding pain of profound loss.

John echoes both Maggie and Darla when he says simply, "Life will *never* be the same."

CHAPTER X

The Spotlight

Don't cry because it's over, smile because it happened.
Dr. Seuss

A MOMENT BEFORE CASTING A fishing line, he was a spring tightly coiled with potential energy, a pure force of nature about to act, a thought made into motion to pierce the boundary between air and water to win the prize.

In the instant before a referee dropped the puck for a face-off, he was poised to attack—to twist, turn, lunge, and speed toward his target, propelling himself and the small cylindrical brick across the ice and toward the chalice.

In June of 2007, Josh Barber was poised in another such moment. He had prepared for years, and yet he still did not know that *this* moment would bring another transformation.

A booking agent had scheduled blues guitarist Jimmie Vaughan and singer Lou Ann Barton for a gig at Lupo's in Providence, Rhode Island, months and months before. Since 1975, this club—originally called Lupo's Heartbreak Hotel—had been showcasing national acts. It would be quite a coup to get a spot on the Jimmie Vaughan bill, and Josh set out to achieve this prize. He had met Vaughan on one of his trips to Austin, Texas, and the two of them hit it off. There was a lot of negotiating, hesitating, and promising before the deal was sealed, but it did happen, and there he was on the poster: "Jimmie Vaughan & Lou Ann Barton, with special guests ROOMFUL OF BLUES, Josh Barber & The Stack. June 26, 2007. Tickets $25. Doors 7:30. Show 8:00."

Josh, Nino, and the guys had been practicing for this opportunity for weeks. They sounded good, felt confident, and were, all-in-all, more than ready. A day or two before the show, Josh's excitement couldn't be contained; he went online to a site hosted by *The Providence Journal* and posted a sample of songs.

Sheila Lennon commented on the afternoon of the concert: "Josh Barber, who's opening tonight at Lupo's for the power lineup of Jimmie Vaughan, Roomful of Blues, and Lou Ann Barton, made a page on our mp3 site last night and uploaded five tunes. If you're going tonight—or wish you were—here's a taste: 'She Knocked Me Down'(mp3)." *Projo Subterranean Homepage News: Bottom-up journalism from the pros: News, tech and culture by Sheila Lennon*

Right about this time, the excitement shifted into anxiety with a crucial bit of bad news: Nino was sick and couldn't get out of bed to perform that night. Josh had a difficult choice to make. The group could go with an all instrumental set that would be competent but not earth-shattering, or he could step up to the microphone and sing. He didn't know what would happen if he chose this option. He sang often for friends and occasionally on stage but never for such an important audience of fans and peers. It was a risk he decided to take.

Josh's emotions were tuned as tightly as his guitar strings when he stepped to center stage directly into the spotlight. His parents and a few friends were in the audience. Young Mike Roberts was looking at him with adulation. The crowd was there for Jimmie, Lou Ann, and Roomful of Blues, but their eagerness for the music was so palpable that Josh caught the spirit and opened up.

The crowd cheered, and he found himself relaxing into the role of lead singer. As he warmed to the enthusiastic attention, his voice emerged in full force, showing its variations and touching every heart in the room. The group played "The Shape I'm In," and two other songs before relinquishing the stage to Roomful of Blues.

Performing had always been magical for Josh but this night had been more than that: it filled him and fulfilled him in quite new ways. It was a graduation of sorts. Josh had emerged quite literally from the shadows into the bright lights and found new dimensions of himself there. He stepped off that stage in June, 2007, with greater confidence, broader shoulders, and a huge smile.

Josh and Jimmie Vaughan, June 26, 2007

PHOTOGRAPHS

Three years old on Kezar Lake

Yantic River, Connecticut – 1983

Uncle Steven, Josh and John on Kezar Lake

Island Life 1987

Josh and Maggie on Kezar Lake – 1988

Josh and Skilo - 1989

**Maggie and Josh at
Mackerel Cove - 1990**

CLCF Hockey - 1991

43 pounder at Zeek's Creek

Three big stripers – Josh, John, and Stevie J.

With his big body guitar

Josh and Yi - 2001

Best Blues Band in RI – 2004

Darla and Josh on the deck 2005

Doyle Bramhall II and Josh Austin Texas - Mid 2000's

URI Graduation 2005 – Yi, Darla, John, Mag, and Josh

Smokestack Lightnin' at the Narragansett Café

Darla and John - 2006

Newport Grande – 2006

Maggie's Pinning Ceremony – 2010

Josh and Mag after Grammy's funeral 2010

Wingman Austin – Spring 2010

Justin and Maggie – September 23, 2011

Darla, John, and Maggie – September 2011

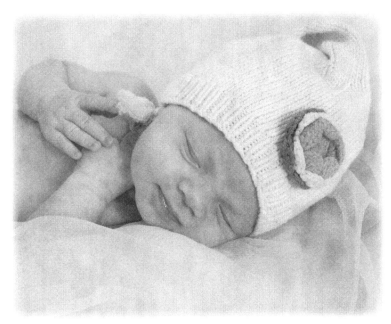

Ava Snow Barber-Leclerc - July 13, 2012

Stevie Ray Vaughan wall mural 1998

Jimi Hendrix wall mural 2010

Stafford Pond wall mural 2009

Self portrait canvas 2010

APPENDIX A

Josh Barber Poems and Song Lyrics

SUN UP, SUN DOWN
Josh Barber

Sun up, Sun down
Time slips away, as the world goes 'round
Bound by a fence, self righteous apprehension
They nod, eyes closed, in silent condescension

He who means no harm to others
Shall walk free amongst his brothers
His life is not theirs, it is his own.

Swallow this now, it'll make you well
It's blind cooperation they seek to sell
We've deemed you unfit to be . . .
You see your free will, has been relieved

He who means no harm to others
Shall walk free amongst his brothers
His life is not theirs, it is his own.

Through this pain you find clarity
Which is dismissed or noted as insanity.
'Subject shows signs of obsession with loss,'
It's therefore our recommendation he remain at any cost.

So left with this moral dilemma,
When rights will be robbed at the decision of others.
But he, who means no harm, shall walk free
Amongst his brothers.

MOVE ON
Josh Barber

So when did it change?
I had feared it as a child, but now it is gone.
It's escape of sweet fate, 'cause we all move on.

How thrilled must you be with this life
To fear the end of your reign?
It's escape of sweet fate, 'cause we all move on.

The fevers would come, and render me numb
The world sped up as I cowered in fear
Is it, they thought, it is this right here?
No, not my fate, but we all move on.

When I was a boy, I fell from an edge.
The ground rose up to meet me instead.
As I staggered around, he found me in a daze.
It was not my fate, although we all move on.

Struck by a stone and left alone, crimson painted the street below
I wasn't far off from that place,
as I felt the heat stream down my face.
But it was not my fate, even though we all move on.

Passing through the thin ice, day becomes night.
Flash of light, reveals your plight.
Don't pull yourself up son, it's worse if you fight!

Out in the distance, their backs are turned
My screams fall short, is it my fate to be learned?
Then just one last roar, one last before I let go.
Their heads turn and now they know.

So it was not my fate, even though we all move on.

I cannot understand the fear you see.
It's just not the same world to me.
Perhaps it's wrong to see fit, wherever it may sit,
But I ponder this sweet fate, 'cause we all move on.

TURN THE PAGE

Josh Barber (posted to Facebook, Tuesday, May 11, 2010, at 4:56 PM)

This ain't the first time; I've read it before
Only then it was me that shut the door
Time heals wounds, I guess we'll see
If not, it's likely the end of me.

For every snarl and every look
There are blank pages within this book
It's only smiles and laughs I see
First it was you, and now it is me.

Some day I'll find those torn out pages
And admit to all the passing phases.
What built up was bound to pop,
And once it did, you could not stop.

The more I pleaded, the more I tried
The more you'd laugh to watch me cry
This pain I felt like none done past
I truly hope it'll be the last.

Your words like razors that cut me deep
There were no nights that I could sleep.
I was then only a shell of a man
Perhaps it was always part of your plan.

Like a tyrant king been overthrown
The peasants mercy would not be shown
For now the weak have become the strong
And they'll pay you back for every wrong.

Your hate fell down on me like rain,

Darla Barber, John Barber, and Magdalena Barber-Leclerc

And I have no words that describe that pain.
You did me in, with all your spite
Others decided against my flight.

Not one, or two, but three are missed
I didn't want it, but you did insist.
The family I knew is now no more
As I lay near death upon this floor.

If left alone it's simple yet clear
This song would not exist, nor would I be here.
Those that loved me bound in haste
And would not let me leave this place.

As time goes by, things will change
Thoughts are constantly rearranged.
I've let you go, you have your way.
No more words you need to say.

Forever life has changed from you.
It comes to mind with all I do.
I will be happy, and live anew.
The same is true for you now, too.

Thank you for all you did while here.
All the love and all the tears.
I think by now you'll know
You meant more to me than I could show.

IN DREAMS

Josh Barber (posted to Facebook, Tuesday, May 11, 2010, at 3:30 PM)
(handwritten note: slow, mellow, Hendrix feel; Bm, F#m)

Staring in the dark, the walls close in
I know the scene well, even before it begins
Wind brings whispers from through the trees
An open window lets them in.

Angels gone to play above
Yet hearts beat on with endless love.
Again sometime I'll see her face
She promises that we'll meet in space.

No time to waste; we don't have long.
There's only so much sand and then it's gone.

Through night we run in fields of bliss
For now is the only time we can kiss
Careful not to trip and fall
To awaken would surely end it all.

Time runs short now, they're calling you home
For now you'll have to be alone.
She says with kindness through falling rain
She knows I'll fight the light in vain.

No time to waste; we don't have long.
There's only so much sand and then it's gone.

She turns her face to feel the breeze
Eyes closed softly yet still she sees
Without a word I'm torn from this place
The look of loss upon my face.

Darla Barber, John Barber, and Magdalena Barber-Leclerc

Again I'll wait for night to come
And return to this place in which she's from

No time to waste; we don't have long.
There's only so much sand and then it's gone.

No time to waste; we don't have long.
There's only so much sand and then it's gone.

TAKE ME HOME

Josh Barber (posted to Facebook, Wednesday, May 5, 2010, 10:35 AM)

As I sit here this morning, see the sun rise above the trees . . .
As I sit here this morning, see the sun rise above the trees . . .
Tell me Mister, where can my woman be?

She done left me, left me all alone . . .
She done left me, left me all alone . . .
She turned her back and said, I don't love you no more.

Tell me woman, where'd you stay last night?
Tell me woman, where'd you stay last night?
Lord I'm fixin', fixin' to start a fight.

When a woman don't love you, she turns cold as ice . . .
When a woman don't love you, she turns cold as ice . . .
She can cut you, deeper than a switchblade knife.
Go away teardrops, take away this pain . . .
Go away teardrops, take away this pain . . .
Lord have mercy, please take me away.

I was ready, standing at the edge . . .
Said I was ready, as I stood at the edge . . .
Heard my Mama pleadin', don't step off that ledge.

Mama, Mama, she done broke my will . . .
Mama, Mama, she done broke my will . . .
You can tell the doctor I don't need no pills.

Well now, take me Lord now, take me way back home . . .
I said, take me Lord now, take me way back home . . .
I had enough and I don't want this life no more.

APPENDIX B

Writings about Josh

FALLING THROUGH THE ICE

Joe Barbera

On a summer night, August 31, 2010,
Josh Barber fell through the ice a second time.
However, this time he did not hold on,
He couldn't.
We so wish he did.

Darla Barber, John Barber, and Magdalena Barber-Leclerc

GETS THE BLUES

For my bluesman and friend, Joshua A Barber
Robert G. Goode, Jr., September 7, 2010

A plastic guitar pick
In the shape of a heart
Lays on the floor

Even a blues man
Gets the blues

He plays and sings
About things
We only dare
to think about

Refuse or unable
to understand

We sit and smoke
what we smoke

We sit and drink
what we drink

If that's
our thing

As we do what we do
we listen to other men

Garden of
sorrows and guilt

As if they
are our own

And to forget
them too

Wish I talked to
my blues man more

Instead of listening
to his notes

If I did
he could still be here
And I
wouldn't have
The forever blues

The heart shape
lays on the floor
surrounded by
darkness.

Darla Barber, John Barber, and Magdalena Barber-Leclerc

Music on a Snowy Night

It was the end of winter 2010 when I listened to the most beautiful music I've ever heard. When I entered the room I heard this music and I was forced to keep listening. The way he strummed his fingers over the guitar strings was amazing. I took a seat next to my brother. The music was smooth; everyone was listening in a daydream because of the soft rhythmic music. Everytime I think of that day it makes me upset because I can only imagine it. I can never relive the sound of the music I heard that snowy winter night.

By Haley Bartlett (age 11)

RESOURCES
AND BIBLIOGRAPHY

THE TWO WEBSITES LISTED BELOW are the best sources of further resources, especially for local chapters of each organization. Books and articles listed below have either been quoted within this book or recommended as helpful by family and others. This is *not* a comprehensive list of resources or information.

Websites

American Foundation for Suicide Prevention (AFSP): "Understanding and preventing suicide through research, education, and advocacy." See http://www.afsp.org/ for local chapters and other information and resources.

National Alliance on Mental Illness (NAMI): The nation's largest grassroots mental health organization. See http://www.nami.org/ for local chapters and other information and resources.

Books and Articles

Baugher, Bob and Jack Jordan. *After Suicide Loss: Coping with Your Grief.* 2002. Available through AFSP.

Bonn, Catherine E. "Suicide and the State: The Ethics of Involuntary Hospitalization for Suicidal Patients." *Intersect* Volume 3, Number 1.

(2010) Accessed online at http://www.stanford.edu/group/publicknowledge/cgi-bin/ojs/sts-journal/index.php/intersect/article/viewFile/197/101.12/16/11.

Butler Hospital E-newsletter. "The Secret Syndrome: Men and Depression." In personal correspondence with PR Department at Butler Hospital.

Greenberg, Gary. *Manufacturing Depression: The Secret History of a Modern Disease.* New York: Simon and Schuster, 2010.

Lanier, Jaron. *You Are Not a Gadget: A Manifesto.* New York: Knopf, 2010.

Mazzotta, Joanne. *Why Whisper: A Memoir.* Xlibris, 2011.

Murray, Albert. *Stomping the Blues.* Cambridge: Da Capo Press, 1989.

Smolin, Ann and John Guinan. *Healing After the Suicide of a Loved One.* New York: Simon and Schuster, 1993.

Solomon, Andrew. *The Noonday Demon: An Atlas of Depression.* New York: Scribner, 2001.

Spiegel, Alix, "When It Comes To Depression, Serotonin Isn't The Whole Story." National Public Radio. January 23, 2012

BOOK GROUP
DISCUSSION QUESTIONS

1. There are some things the Barber family could not know and will never know about their son. What do you think remains unknown for this family? What remains unknown for you? If you are unable to have clear answers to your questions, how do you move forward? What is healing for you?

2. Which of Josh's journal entries, songs, and poems did you find most moving to read? Why?

3. Consider the roles of parents and a sibling in this book. Write a message to Darla or to John or to Maggie to let them know your thoughts.

4. Emergency systems are established by communities to help people who are experiencing a crisis when there is no one else to turn to. When did this family turn to emergency responders and facilities, and how did they feel about this?

5. Think about the chapter of this book called "We All Move On," where the family members comment on how they are doing up to several years later. How has your own grief changed or progressed since the time of your loss? Consider writing a short "epilogue" as if it is part of a book about your experiences.

6. Thinking about your own loss, how has your relationship with your loved one been maintained or preserved since her or his death?

CPSIA information can be obtained at www.ICGtesting.com
Printed in the USA
BVOW04*0457190913

331553BV00001B/2/P